שָׁלוֹם וּבְרָכָה

THE NEW HEBREW PRIMER

TEACHER'S EDITION

By

Ari Y. Goldberg

Education Consultants

Gila Gevirtz

Sarah Gluck

Terry S. Kaye

Wendy B. Rosen

Ruby G. Strauss

Jessica B. Weber

BEHRMAN HOUSE

TABLE OF CONTENTS

Copyright © 1999 Behrman House, Inc.

Published by Behrman House, Inc.

West Orange, NJ 07052

ISBN: 0-87441-678-7

MANUFACTURED IN THE UNITED STATES OF AMERICA

Teacher's Edition Design: Itzhack Shelomi

Black-Line Masters Illustrations: Larry Nolte

TO THE TEACHER

You are a reading teacher. For a few moments, put yourself in the place of the student. The language you will learn consists of only eight graphic symbols. They are printed here with their English equivalents.

⊠	=	A
⍺	=	B
⍺	=	D
○	=	E
❄	=	H
★	=	I
□	=	R
☺	=	W

Study this alphabet for a few minutes. When you are finished, continue reading.

Now try to read this sentence.

Do you need more time? Do you need more help? Imagine doing this exercise with many more letters added and after a lapse of several days between studying the letters and decoding them. Hard, isn't it? Yet the task we set for our students is even more difficult.

You have been entrusted with a challenging and important job: to help your students read Hebrew. *Shalom Uvrachah—The New Hebrew Primer* will make your job easier, more pleasant, and much more successful.

Because of individual differences, some children will require more practice, help, and time than others. *Shalom Uvrachah* provides the variety of opportunities necessary for every child to learn to read Hebrew.

INTENT AND PURPOSE OF *SHALOM UVRACHAH*

The purpose of *Shalom Uvrachah—The New Hebrew Primer* is to teach Hebrew decoding skills while transmitting Jewish values and beliefs.

Each of the 25 Lessons introduces a carefully chosen Jewish cultural word—the key word—that enriches the student's cultural vocabulary while the student gradually develops a series of meaningful Hebrew decoding skills. In some cases, the key word may spark recognition of a concept from the student's background. This recognition will contribute to the student's sense of belonging to and feeling part of our rich Jewish cultural heritage. The key words, such as *mezuzah*, *baruch*, *mitzvah*, and *emet*, also serve as clues to help the student recall letter-sound and vowel-sound associations.

Based upon recent studies of Hebrew teaching methods, confusing letters are introduced separately and vowel sounds are carefully and systematically introduced in small manageable portions. Reading exercises provide extensive practice opportunity for each consonant and vowel. Numerous meaningful and challenging activities (e.g., Mix and Match, Name Know-How) offer additional learning opportunities for reading, writing, and exploring the Jewish cultural concepts.

Following is a brief outline of the text's components:

1. letter-sound association
2. vowel-sound association
3. visual discrimination
4. look-alike letters
5. sound-alike vowels
6. diagnostic evaluations
7. Jewish cultural enrichment

Shalom Uvrachah has been designed to ease your students through the acquisition of Hebrew reading skills—to inspire and encourage them to want to learn more, and to instill in them a sense of pride and joy in the acquisition of a Jewish cultural vocabulary.

HOW TO USE THE TEXTBOOK

Using the Teacher's Edition

This Teacher's Edition contains the entire text of the *Shalom Uvrachah* textbook, reproduced in reduced size. The pages are annotated with suggested activities, teaching methods, and other information to assist you. Various black-line masters that supplement the material in this Teacher's Edition are also provided following page xx.

Keep in mind that students learn in different ways. The three primary ways are aural, visual, and tactile. Similarly, teachers teach in different ways. Don't feel obligated to use a method that does not feel comfortable with your teaching style. By the same token, remember that since students learn in different ways, you should vary your teaching methods. Feel free to repeat an activity or method that worked especially well for you and your students.

> The information and suggestions in this Teacher's Edition are intended to assist you in developing your own teaching plan. You do not need to follow every suggestion on every page. Rather, many different options are provided from which you can choose.

Pacing

Students differ in ability. Teachers differ in style. Schools differ in the number of class sessions scheduled each week. Ultimately, you must decide how to pace your class's progress through the text.

The lessons in *Shalom Uvrachah* vary in length. Some lessons may take only one class session to cover, while others may take several sessions. A short, but more difficult, lesson may take more time to teach than a longer, simpler, lesson.

Remember that the mastery of each new letter or vowel is what is most important. Before advancing to a new lesson, each student should be able to read aloud all the letters and vowels learned in previous lessons, know their names, and be able to blend the sounds. Feel free to go back to previous lessons to review a letter or vowel whenever you feel the need to do so.

Homework

Whether or not to give homework is a question that should be addressed to your school principal. Keep in mind that homework can provide students with the additional contact, repetition, and reinforcement of what has already been learned in class. Homework should not be used as a tool to teach new information.

If you do give homework, *Shalom Uvrachah* makes assigning homework easy. Built into each lesson are a variety of exercises that reinforce reading skills. Any one of these exercises can be completed for homework.

Be sure to review homework assignments during the following class session. Doing this reassures the students that their efforts were noted and were a worthwhile expenditure of time.

Family Education

A partnership between home and school can help your students reach their greatest potential in their Hebrew studies. Therefore, every effort should be made to facilitate this partnership with your students' parents. Several special black-line masters are included in this Teacher's Edition to aid you in this endeavor.

- Send home a letter after the first class session to establish parent-teacher communication. A sample is provided.
- You can also send home the illustrated *alef-bet* chart. Ask the parents to post it on the refrigerator so the student can mark off each letter after it has been learned.

Make sure to include the parents in a *Siyum Hasefer* celebration (see page xx) when the students have finished learning all the letters.

SCOPE AND SEQUENCE

The chart below shows the order of letter and vowel introduction in *Shalom Uvrachah*. You will note that the letters are not introduced in alphabetical sequence but are based upon the presentation of key cultural terms. Vowel sounds have been carefully and systematically introduced in small manageable portions.

Lesson Number	Text Page	Key Word	Letters	Vowels
1	4	שַׁבָּת	ב ת ת שׁ	ָ
2	12	שֶׁמֶשׁ	מ	
3	16	כַּלָה	ל כ ה	
4	24	בְּרָכָה	ר כ	ְ
5	31	הַבְדָלָה	ב ד	ַ
6	38	וְאָהַבְתָ	א ו	
7	44	צְדָקָה	ק צ	
8	52	מִצְוָה		ִי
9	56	שְׁמַע	ע	
10	61	נָבִיא	נ ן	
11	66	חַלָה	ח	
12	71	עֲלִיָה	י	
13	75	לְחַיִים	ם	
14	81	תּוֹרָה		וֹ

Lesson Number	Text Page	Key Word	Letters	Vowels
15	86	טַלִית	ט	
16	92	אֱמֶת		ֱ ֶ
17	97	פֶּסַח	פּ ס	
18	103	שׁוֹפָר	פ	
19	108	עֵץ חַיִים	ץ	ֵי
20	114	יִשְׂרָאֵל	שׂ	
21	119	חַג שָׂמֵחַ	ג	
22	127	קָדוֹשׁ		וּ
23	132	מְזוּזָה	ז	
24	138	בָּרוּךְ	ך	
25	143	אָלֶף	ף	
Special Rules	148			
Selected Readings	152			

Vowels

There are opposing opinions regarding whether or not the *names* of the vowels should be taught. The decision about whether to teach the vowel names should be guided by your school policy.

You will note that the pronunciation of vowel *sounds* is not formally taught in the book. This is so because there is not universal agreement about the exact pronunciation of some of the Hebrew vowels. Therefore, it is left up to each school to teach the vowel sounds according to its practice and tradition.

Your students may wonder why there is another version of the *pataḥ* and *segol* vowels. Four letters in the Hebrew alphabet (ע ח ה א) cannot take a *shvah* at the beginning of a word or syllable because of the difficulty in pronunciation; instead they take on "helping" vowels to enable the reader to pronounce the syllable (e.g., הֲלָכָה).

The development of grammatical rules such as this show how sensible the grammarians were in adapting Hebrew to the needs and abilities of those who were reading and speaking it.

Vowel Name	Vowel
kamatz	ָ
pataḥ	ַ
shvah	ְ
ḥataf pataḥ	ֲ
ḥirik	ִי ִ
ḥolam	ֹ וֹ
segol	ֶ
ḥataf segol	ֱ
tsere	ֵי ֵ
shuruk	וּ
kubutz	ֻ

TEACHING AIDS

Chalkboard

Use the chalkboard to introduce new letters, to drill the class on letter combinations, to demonstrate similarities and differences between letters, to answer questions, to play games, and to present assignments.

Remember to vary the way in which you use the chalkboard. This can be as simple as changing the chalk color or varying the size of the letters you write.

Draw a picture on the chalkboard to illustrate the lesson. (The less polished an artist you are, the more the class will love your drawings.)

Incorporate children's need for physical movement. Plan quick-paced exercises that involve coming to the board. For example, have students copy a word that you have written on the chalkboard. There is really nothing more special about writing on a chalkboard than on paper—unless you are a child. Coming to the front of the room and writing on the chalkboard is exciting to many students. If they enjoy using the chalkboard, let them do it.

Flannelboard

A flannelboard can be used with the entire class, with small groups, or by a single student. It saves writing time at the chalkboard and presents letters exactly as they appear in a printed book. It also offers students the opportunity to manipulate letters and to form whole words.

Flannelboards can be purchased at a school supplies store or may be easily constructed by covering a large piece of cardboard with flannel. You can make flannelboard letters by gluing a small piece of velcro or sandpaper onto the back of existing flashcards or by cutting flashcards out of rough-textured construction paper. Most flannelboard techniques will also work with a magnetic board.

The flannelboard can be used to introduce new letters and display them clearly. It is also useful for drill or review.

Alef-Bet Chart

The *alef-bet* chart reminds the class that its ultimate goal is to learn the *alef-bet*. Consider displaying several different *alef-bet* charts to enhance the feeling that Hebrew is an important aspect of the classroom routine.

Use the chart to introduce new letters, to compare the appearance of letters, and to demonstrate the progress the class has made.

Point to individual letters on the chart. Go around the room and have each child, in turn, pronounce the name and sound of the letter.

Say the sound of a Hebrew letter and ask a student to point to the letter or letters that have that sound, or say the name of a Hebrew letter and ask a student to point to the correct letter.

Select two students. Have one say the sound of a letter and the other point to the letter that has that sound.

Alef-Bet Flashcards

The clue to the most effective use of flashcards lies in their name— flash. How long is a flash? At first, a flash can take a long time. Our goal is not to reach any specific speed but to increase the given speed gradually. Flashcard drills are effective and their very pace can make them exciting, but like all drills, they can become boring. Variety helps to maintain interest.

Here are some additional ways to use the *alef-bet* flashcards:

1. Hold the cards facing you and turn them around one at a time. Have each child identify the name and sound of the letter. Shuffle the cards and repeat, beginning with a different child, so that each child is given a turn with a new letter. Give each child

several turns. For variety, after flashing for name and sounds separately, vary requests at random: e.g., name, name, sound, name, sound.

2. Put the cards into a bag and have each child take a turn fishing out a letter and giving its name or sound.

3. Distribute cards to each student. As you call out a name or sound, the student with the matching card holds it up.

4. Draw a tic-tac-toe grid on the chalkboard. Divide the class into two teams. Display a flashcard to team *alef*. If a student from team *alef* answers correctly, the student may write an *alef* in a square. Students from team *bet* do the same, using a *bet*. Keep playing until one team has three *alefs* or *bets* in a row. A "tournament" can be created by awarding the winning team one point. A new grid is drawn, and the game continues as long as you like.

5. Use a baseball theme. A correct answer to a displayed flashcard gets a team to first base. An incorrect answer is an out. A team with four correct answers has scored a run.

6. Distribute one flashcard to each student. Have students read their card silently and then hold it up. The first student, who has been given, let us say, a *gimmel*, says, "I packed my grandmother's suitcase, and in it I put a *gimmel*." The next student, who has been given a *bet*, says, "I packed my grandmother's suitcase, and in it I put a *gimmel* and a *bet*." The game continues in this manner. After everyone has had a chance, repeat the game but start in a different direction so those who had a few letters to read now have many. On this second round, students should be encouraged to quicken the tempo.

7. Display letter and vowel flashcards #1–7 on the chalkboard ledge. Say, "I spy a *bet*" or "I spy an *'ah'* sound." Call on a student to come up and point to the card you "spied." Upon selecting the correct card, the student now has a turn to "spy" a card. The student then calls on a classmate to come up and find it.

Student Flashcards

Each student can make his or her own set of *alef-bet* flashcards. Black-line masters for student flashcards are provided in this Teacher's Edition following page xx. Once duplicated, the sheets can be cut apart and mounted on index cards for classroom use or home practice. Provide each student with a storage envelope. This can be stapled to the inside cover of the text.

Word Cards

There is a set of word cards available for use with *Shalom Uvrachah*. These cards, printed on durable, heavy cardboard, include all Key and Heritage words covered by the book. (Each word card is numbered for easy reference to activities included in this Teacher's Edition.) The English meaning is on the back of each word card.

Word cards may be used by individuals or small groups of students, or by the class as a whole. Use the word cards to introduce the Key and Heritage words in each Lesson. Also use the word cards for review.

1. Display a number of word cards on the edge of the chalkboard or in a pocket chart. Provide a clue about one of the words and have the student read the correct word. For example, "This is the Jewish state" – *Yisrael*.

2. Distribute word cards to the class. Call out, one at a time, the words and phrases found on the individual cards. The student with the matching card supplies the correct answer by standing up, displaying the card, and reading the word or phrase.

3. Make a packet of ten word cards. The students sit or stand in a circle and pass the packet around while music is played on a tape or CD player. (Try to use Jewish or Israeli music.) When the

music stops, the student holding the packet reads and/or translates the top card. This card is then placed at the bottom of the pile and the game continues in the same fashion.

4. Post two columns of word cards with six cards in each column. Individuals or teams choose a column. Taking turns, the students read the six Hebrew words. Then they switch and read the words in the other column. You can also play the game by translating the words.

5. Post a column of at least six words. Individuals or teams take turns "climbing up the ladder" by reading and translating the words on the ladder. Score one point for each word read correctly and two points for each word translated correctly. Then play again by reading the words in the opposite order to climb down the ladder.

6. Double sets of word cards (two identical cards for each word) can be used to play a memory game. After shuffling the cards, lay out sixteen cards (eight pairs of words) upside down, in rows. A student picks a card and reads it. He or she then tries to find its match. If successful, the student must then tell the meaning of the word in order to keep the pair. If the student defines the word incorrectly, or doesn't find the matching card, then the initial card is returned to its place face down.

Stopwatch and Tape Recorder

A stopwatch is an easy way to assess improvement in reading fluency. It can be used to time the speed at which a student reads a passage. Many students enjoy the experience of competing against their own best time.

The tape recorder also provides students with proof of their improvement. Record students as they read through a passage. Two or three weeks later have the students, in the same order, read the passage on a second tape. Then play back both and compare.

ALEF-BET FLASHCARDS AND WORD CARDS – MASTER LIST

A set of *alef-bet* flashcards and word cards are available for use with *Shalom Uvrachah*.
Each card is numbered for ease of use with this Teacher's Edition.

Word Cards

שִׂמְחַת תּוֹרָה 61	הַמּוֹצִיא לֶחֶם 41	שְׁמַע 21	שַׁבָּת 1
חַג שָׂמֵחַ 62	אֲרוֹן הַקֹּדֶשׁ 42	עִבְרִית 22	בַּת 2
הַגָּדָה 63	אֱלֹהִים 43	נָבִיא 23	שֶׁמֶשׁ 3
מְגִילָה 64	פֶּסַח 44	חַלָּה 24	כַּלָּה 4
מָגֵן דָּוִד 65	כִּפָּה 45	הָרַחֲמָן 25	שַׁבָּת הַכַּלָּה 5
מָשִׁיחַ 66	מִשְׁפָּחָה 46	עֲלִיָּה 26	בְּרָכָה 6
קָדוֹשׁ 67	חֶסֶד 47	מִנְיָן 27	מַלְכָּה 7
סִדּוּר 68	שׁוֹפָר 48	לְחַיִּים 28	שַׁבָּת הַמַּלְכָּה 8
יְהוּדִים 69	נֶפֶשׁ 49	אָדָם 29	הַבְדָּלָה 9
חֻמָשׁ 70	תְּפִילָּה 50	יְצִיאַת מִצְרַיִם 30	וְאָהַבְתָּ 10
יְרוּשָׁלַיִם 71	הַפְטָרָה 51	תּוֹרָה 31	אַהֲבָה 11
אֵלִיָּהוּ הַנָּבִיא 72	אֲפִיקוֹמָן 52	שַׁבָּת שָׁלוֹם 32	צְדָקָה 12
מְזוּזָה 73	עֵץ חַיִּים 53	הַמּוֹצִיא 33	קַבָּלַת שַׁבָּת 13
מַחֲזוֹר 74	סֵדֶר 54	רֹאשׁ הַשָּׁנָה 34	מַצָּה 14
מַזָּל טוֹב 75	אָמֵן 55	קִדּוּשׁ 35	מִצְוָה 15
בָּרוּךְ 76	סֵפֶר תּוֹרָה 56	שָׁלוֹם 36	בַּר מִצְוָה 16
מֶלֶךְ 77	נֵר תָּמִיד 57	טַלִּית 37	בַּת מִצְוָה 17
אָלֶף 78	חָמֵץ 58	יוֹם טוֹב 38	צִיצִית 18
אָלֶף בֵּית 79	יִשְׂרָאֵל 59	שָׁנָה טוֹבָה 39	קַדִּישׁ 19
חַי 80	עֲשֶׂרֶת הַדִּבְּרוֹת 60	אֱמֶת 40	הַתִּקְוָה 20

Alef-Bet Flashcards

ג 41	ָ 21	בּ 1
וּ 42	י 22	תּ 2
֗ 43	ע 23	ת 3
ז 44	נ 24	שׁ 4
ך 45	ז 25	יְ 5
ף 46	ח 26	ָ 6
	י 27	מ 7
	ם 28	ל 8
	ו 29	כּ 9
	30	ה 10
	ט 31	ר 11
	ֵ 32	כ 12
	ֶ 33	ִ 13
	פ 34	ב 14
	ס 35	ד 15
	פ 36	ֹ 16
	37	א 17
	י 38	ו 18
	ץ 39	ק 19
	שׂ 40	צ 20

TEACHING STRATEGIES

Key Words and Heritage Words

The words in *Shalom Uvrachah* have been specifically chosen because they transmit some of the values and beliefs of our Jewish heritage.

Introducing real words to the students is important because it assures them that learning Hebrew is more than just a process of decoding symbols.

Each lesson in *Shalom Uvrachah* contains a "Key Word," accompanied by an illustration representing the Key word at the top of the opening page. The Key word and related concepts are explained at the end of the Lesson in a section entitled, "The Living Tradition." You should have the students discuss these concepts in some detail. A photograph related to the Key word prefaces each of "The Living Tradition" sections. To facilitate discussion of the concepts related to the Key word, this Teacher's Edition contains guiding questions to be asked of the students when "Using the Photograph."

Additional "Heritage Words" are also included in each lesson. These enrich the students' study of Hebrew by introducing words which demonstrate that Hebrew is an integral part of Judaic study and being a Jew. You should not spend a significant amount of time discussing the Heritage words and their related concepts. However, the students should have a basic familiarity with them.

Word cards containing both the Key and Heritage words can be a valuable tool for teaching new letters or vowels, facilitating drill work, and discussing concepts related to the Jewish cultural words. In addition, this Teacher's Edition provides supplemental exercises and activities to expand the students' understanding of the Key and Heritage words.

Here are some techniques for using the Key word to teach new letters and vowels:

1. Display the word card representing the Key word, write the Key word on the chalkboard, or have the students look at the Key word in their textbooks and then read the word to the class. If the students are familiar with any of the letters or vowels in the word, have the students identify them.
2. Discuss concepts related to the Key word and then point out the new letter or vowel being introduced.
3. If only one new letter or vowel is being introduced in the lesson, read the Key word to the students and ask the students to guess the sound of the new letter or vowel.
4. When using the textbook, have the students point to the new letter or vowel in the Key word.

New Letter and Vowel Introduction

Here are some techniques for introducing new letters and vowels:

1. Write the new letter on the chalkboard in print form.
2. Put the new letter on the flannelboard or magnetic board.
3. Pronounce the name and sound of the new letter or vowel and have the class repeat it in unison or individually.
4. Have students point to the new letter on the *alef-bet* chart and pronounce it.
5. When introducing a new letter, write a vowel the class already knows under the letter and ask the class to pronounce what you have written. Erase and change the vowels until you have used all the vowels the class knows. You can also follow a similar procedure using the flannelboard or magnetic board.
6. When introducing a new vowel, follow the procedure noted in #5 but instead combine the new vowel with different familiar letters.
7. Stress visual similarities with and differences from other letters or vowels.
8. Have the students form the letters or vowels out of pretzel sticks or licorice strips, and then enjoy the treat. You can also use nonedible materials such as pipe cleaners, yarn, ribbon, etc.

After you have introduced the new letter or vowel, have the students open their books to the new lesson. It is recommended that you introduce and practice the new letter or vowel before turning to the text, because children think of reading as something done from a book. If the difficult task of learning new material is done by using other teaching aids, then the task of reading—using the textbook—will be more rewarding.

Reading Techniques

There is no substitute for reading drill. The only way to produce fluent readers is to have them read and read, and then read some more.

If the class has read a page accurately, review the material with an eye toward increasing speed. If the class cannot read a page accurately, have them read it a second or third time. As a reminder to do this, every page of standard reading drill is prefaced by the phrase "Now Read & Read Again," along with the use of the recycling symbol.

Here are some techniques for making reading practice more interesting and varied in your classroom:

1. **Pairs**. Have students work in pairs reading lines to each other. Match a stronger reader with a weaker reader. Listen as they practice, correcting any errors that you hear.

2. **Random Selection**. Let the student roll a die or pick a number out of a hat. Whichever number comes up is the line the student must read.

3. **Songs**. Have the students try singing the sounds to the tune of a simple song such as "Twinkle Twinkle Little Star" or "Mary Had a Little Lamb." This works best with simple, single-syllable sounds.

4. **Echo Reading**. Divide the class into two groups, choosing from a variety of criteria: boys/girls; students with birthdays before July/after July; students wearing red/no red. One group is "reader" and the other is "echo." "Reader" reads a word or group of words and "echo" repeats the same word or words. Repeat the activity but switch "reader" and "echo."

5. **Tic-Tac-Toe**. Draw a tic-tac-toe grid on the chalkboard. Divide the class into two teams. To place an X or an O on the board, the students must correctly read a line in the book.

6. **Staccato Interruption**. Have a child read until you clap your hands. At that time, the next student reads. Determine the number of words according to the student's ability and reading fluency, keeping the pace lively.

7. **Choral Reading**. Have the first row of students read the first line in unison. Have the second row read the second line, and so on until all the lines have been read.

8. **Timed Reading**. Use a stopwatch to time reading. Students enjoy competing against their own best time.

9. **Student's Choice**. Allow each student the opportunity to read one line of his or her choice. Have them identify the line number before reading. Another version is to have one student read a line and then call out another line number for the next student to read, or call out the name of the next reader.

10. **Team Reading**. Have four students work together to correct each other as members of the group take turns reading complete lines.

11. **Special Attention Words**. Call out a specific word, such as "line 3, fourth word," and have a child read that word. Have the child call out the location of the next one, or continue to call them out yourself with emphasis on words or letter that need extra attention.

12. **Responsive Reading**. Have students take turns reading one phrase at a time, with the class responding in unison.

13. **Odds and Evens**. Change the line sequence by first reading all the odd-numbered lines followed by the even-numbered lines.

14. **Finger Follow-Along**. Encourage students to concentrate by following the reading with their fingers.

15. **Stay Alert**. Keep students on their toes by calling on the same child more than once.

16. **Overlapping Words**. Have students read three words at a time. The first student reads three words. The second student overlaps by reading three words beginning with the second word. The third student begins with the third word, and so on. Another variation is to have the student begin with the previous student's last word.

17. **What's Missing**? Have one student read all the Hebrew sounds or words on a line, omitting one. Another student reads the sound or word that was skipped.

18. **Tape Recording**. Record students as they read a line. Two or three weeks later have the students read the same line, in the same order, on a second tape. Play back both tapes and compare.

19. **Dramatic Reading**. There was once a famous actress who was so talented that she was able to bring tears to the eyes of an audience simply by reciting the alphabet. Instruct the students to read a line of syllables dramatically, as if they were on stage. For example, suggest to the first person to read the line angrily; the second person should read sadly, and so on. A variation of this is to whisper a situation to the reader (e.g., you have just won a million dollars) and the class must guess the emotion the reader is trying to convey.

Writing Pages

Demonstrate on the chalkboard the shape of the letter and the direction in which you form it, explaining what you are doing as you do it. Ask the class to draw the letter in the air. Have volunteers come to the board to write the letter. Using the blank lines in the book, direct the students to write the parts of each letter one stroke at a time. As the students write the letter in their books, walk around the classroom to check that they are writing correctly.

Shalom Uvrachah is printed in two editions—one that teaches manuscript print writing and the other that teaches cursive script writing. This Teacher's Edition is universal and can be used with either student edition.

A chart of all the Hebrew letters, along with examples of how each is handwritten in script format, is on the next page. Print writing examples can be seen in this Teacher's Edition on the writing practice pages of the reduced size page from the student primer.

HEBREW SCRIPT WRITING SAMPLES

	Script Format	Letter			Script Format	Letter
ג‍	lc	א		ס‍	ס	מ
ڑ ڑ	ב ב	ב ב		ן‍	ן	נ ן
�<	<	ג		ן‍	ן	ס
ؤ‍	ؤ	ד		O‍	O	ע
ה‍	ה	ה		פ‍ פ‍	פ‍ פ	פ ף
ו‍	ו	ו		۶‍	۶	צ ץ
ل‍	ל	ז		۶‍	۶	ק
ה‍	ח	ח		ק‍	ק	ר
ט‍	ט	ט י		ר‍	ר	ש שׁ
،‍	،	י		ﻉ‍ ﻉ‍	ﻉ ﻉ	ת ת
כ‍ כ‍	כ כ	כ ך		ﻖ‍ ﻖ‍	ﻖ	
ך‍	ך	ל				
ؤ‍	ؤ	ל				
N‍	N	מ				

xiv

Remediation

What should you do to remedy reading problems? The strategy that you use depends upon the specific nature of the problem.

When students mispronounce words...

Read the word and have the class repeat ("echo") it.

Read the word again, slowly decoding each letter and vowel part.

When students are not reading fluently...

Have the students read into a tape recorder.

Tape-record a page and have individual students read along.

Use a stopwatch to encourage reading fluency.

When students lack confidence in reading...

Assign classmates for peer tutoring.

Group students of varying abilities together.

Encourage parental assistance.

When classwide errors occur...

Reteach the material.

Offer more class drill.

Reassess your teaching method.

When motivation to improve is needed...

Offer praise and encouragement.

Allow the students to act as teacher for a few minutes.

Give out stickers or small prizes.

Communicate with parents.

TIME MANAGEMENT

How to complete the book in one school year, teaching one Lesson (or chapter) per week.

We recommend that your students spend a full year learning to read. Fluency and accuracy in Hebrew reading are important to their future success in Hebrew language study and to their sense of achievement in religious school.

One of the most difficult things to do when planning a curriculum is deciding exactly how to use the class time. The following charts are designed to help you decide how to allocate the time available. Each class session should be divided into at least four distinct components.

1. Opening activity to review previous material or to set up the class session
2. Introduction of new material
3. Reinforcement of new material
4. Closing activity to summarize and reinforce the class session's content

The amount of time spent on each component will depend on the overall amount of time available for Hebrew instruction and on what you wish to accomplish. Completing a Lesson Plan Form (included in the black-line master section of this book) in advance of every class session will help you to manage your time so that all your goals can be met.

If You Meet Once a Week for Hebrew Instruction...

If your school meets once a week for thirty weeks, on average you will need to complete one Lesson per week. Keep in mind that some Lessons will introduce two or three letters, while others will introduce only one. Therefore, some Lessons will require more than one week

of study, while other weeks you may be able to cover two Lessons in one class session.

If You Meet Twice a Week for Hebrew Instruction...

If your school meets twice a week for thirty weeks, you can spend approximately two classroom sessions per Lesson. Again, you will need to take into consideration the number of letters or vowels introduced in each Lesson and pace your class accordingly.

SAMPLE CLASS SESSIONS (50 MINUTES)

Lesson 6 of *Shalom Uvrachah* teaches two letters – *alef* and *vav.* You will probably need two class sessions to teach this Lesson. Here are sample outlines for the class sessions teaching these letters. Remember that detailed teaching instructions page are included in this Teacher's Edition.

Lesson 6, pages 38–40, *alef*

Activity	Purpose	Examples	Time
Opening Activity • Review • Warm-up • Motivational Introduction	Reinforce previous learning; Provoke interest in new material	**Review:** Drill letters and vowels learned, using *alef-bet* flashcard "Go Fish" game. Put cards #1–16 into a bag and have each child take a turn fishing out a letter and giving its name and/or sound.	10 min.
Introduction of New Material • Key Word • Letter	Provide context to Hebrew studies and motivation to learn new material; Present core curriculum material	**Key Word:** What prayer tells us to love God? Why should we love God? Sing the Ve'ahavta paragraph together if your students know it. Display word card (#10). Read the word. **Teaching the New Letter:** Display the *alef* flash card (#17). Ask a student to point out the *alef* on the *alef-bet* chart. Ensure that the students understand the concept of a letter that is not sounded.	15 min.
Reinforcement • Reading • Heritage Words	Refine reading accuracy and fluency; Reinforce new material; Provide context to Hebrew studies	**Reading Practice** [Page 38]: Before reading, have the students look at the key word in the textbook and point to the *alef.* Call on students to read lines 1–3. The class repeats these lines in unison. **Now Read & Read Again** [Page 39]: Students work in pairs reading the lines to each other. **Heritage Words** [Page 39]: Ask the students to make a list of things that they love. Is God on the list? What things are common to most of the students' lists?	20 min.
Closing Activity • Exercise	Provides reinforcement	**Exercise** [Page 40]: The teacher reads aloud the name of the Hebrew letter in each box and the students circle the matching Hebrew letter on that line.	5 min.

Lesson 6, pages 40–43, *vav*

Activity	Purpose	Examples	Time
Introduction of New Material • Key Word • Letter	Provide context to Hebrew studies and motivation to learn new material; Present core curriculum material	**Teaching the New Letter:** Display word card #10 (וְאָהַבְתָּ). Ask a student to name all the letters, except for the first. Read the word to the students and review its meaning. Point to the first letter and introduce the name and sound of the *vav*. Have a student point to the *vav* on the *alef-bet* chart. Using the chalkboard or flannelboard, review letters similar to the *vav*.	10 min.
Reinforcement • Reading • Heritage Words	Refine reading accuracy and fluency; Reinforce new material; Provide context to Hebrew studies	**Reading Practice** [Page 40]: Call on a student to read line 1. The class repeats the lines in unison. Repeat this procedure with lines 2 and 3. **Now Read & Read Again** [Page 41]: Change the line sequence by first reading all the odd-numbered lines followed by the even-numbered lines. Don't forget to recycle!	15 min.
Introduction of New Material • Writing Practice • Word Find	Present core curriculum material	**Write the Letters** [Page 42]: On the chalkboard, demonstrate the technique for writing the letter *alef.* Repeat it several times. Have the students write the letter *alef* with in the ruled lines provided in the textbook. Repeat this procedure the *vav*. **Write the Words** [Page 42]: Write the word *ahavah* on the chalkboard. Then call on a few students to come to the chalkboard to write the word. The other students should write the word *ahavah* in the space provided in the book. Repeat this procedure with the word *ve'ahavta*. **Word Find** Have the students complete this exercise independantly.	15 min.
Closing Activity • Using the Photograph • Think About It	Provides reinforcement of key words	**Using the Photograph** [Page 43]: Ask the students: What book do you think the boy is reading? Why do you think so? **Think About It** [Page 43]: Read the translation of the Ve'ahavta paragraph. What does it mean to love God with all your heart, soul, and might? By performing *mitzvot* are we showing love for God? Why or why not?	10 min.

THE FIRST DAY OF SCHOOL

Setting the Stage

Before the first day of school, spend time planning the appearance of your classroom. The classroom should convey the message that Hebrew is exciting and important and that studying and learning Hebrew will be pleasant, worthwhile, and fun.

Play recordings of Israeli songs. Hang *alef-bet* charts and attractive Hebrew posters around the room. Display a selection of Hebrew books or anything else that contains Hebrew letters. Label classroom objects with their Hebrew names. Try to include both items of a religious nature (e.g., a haggadah, a ḥallah cover), as well as items from Israeli popular culture (e.g., soda labels, comic books). The appearance of your classroom is an important motivation for learning.

Introducing the Hebrew Language

Tell the students that they will be learning to read a language that is both very old and very new. The Torah, Judaism's oldest and holiest document, is written in Hebrew. Most of our prayers are written in Hebrew. But Hebrew is also a very new language. Up until the late 1800s, Hebrew was used only for ritual purposes. As the result of the creation of the State of Israel and the adoption of Hebrew as Israel's official language, Hebrew has come to be used as a living, everyday language. For further information, *Journey Through Jewish History* by Seymour Rossel, available from Behrman House, has a section (pages 117–118) relating the amazing story of the father of modern Hebrew, Eliezer ben Yehudah, and the rebirth of the Hebrew language.

Hebrew Is Read from Right to Left

Demonstrate how to open a Hebrew book. Ask a student to come up and find the first page in a Hebrew book. Open a Hebrew book and point to where we begin reading on a page. Have an English and Hebrew phrase written on the chalkboard. Ask a student to come to the board and point to where one would begin to read each phrase.

Introducing the Textbook

Explain that in Judaism when we begin something new we say a special thank you to God by reciting a blessing. This blessing is called the Sheheḥeyanu. Lead the class in the recitation of the blessing.

בָּרוּךְ אַתָּה ה׳ אֱלֹהֵינוּ מֶלֶךְ הָעוֹלָם,
שֶׁהֶחֱיָנוּ וְקִיְּמָנוּ וְהִגִּיעָנוּ לַזְּמַן הַזֶּה.

Baruch atah Adonai Eloheinu melech ha'olam, sheheḥeyanu v'kiy'manu v'higiyanu lazman hazeh.

Praised are You, Adonai our God, Ruler of the universe, who has kept us in life, sustained us, and enabled us to reach this season.

Distribute the textbooks. Show the students the Hebrew letters on the cover. Allow a minute for the students to examine their new books, to flip through the pages, and to enjoy the colorful design. Then ask the students to open the book the "Hebrew way." Check to see that this is done properly.

Explain that there is a custom of eating something sweet on the first day of school so that learning will be a sweet and happy experience. Arrange to have candy, raisins, or other sweets to distribute to each child. Consider also having other treats, such as pretzels or popcorn, for students who may have special dietary concerns.

Tell the students that by the end of the year, they will be able to follow along in the *siddur* (prayerbook) and *ḥumash* (Five Books of Moses) during Synagogue services because they will know all the letters and vowels in the *alef-bet*!

Homework

The beginning of school is often a time of enthusiasm for the students, so now is the time when students are most eager to do homework. If you plan to assign homework throughout the year, give an assignment on the first day. This will also create the understanding and expectation that homework will be a regular part of their Hebrew learning experience.

Parent Participation

When parents are informed, students become more involved. When children sense their parents' interest, they become more motivated to achieve. We have prepared a sample letter which can be found in the black-line master section of this book, that you can send home to parents, which tells them about the important part they can play in their child's Hebrew studies. It will also help you establish positive parent-teacher communication.

FYI

Some of your students may have had previous exposure to the Hebrew alphabet. Your students' Hebrew backgrounds need not affect your teaching methods, although they may affect how you pace the lessons.

SIYUM HASEFER
(Completing the Book)

When the class has finished *Shalom Uvrachah*, it is time for a celebration. It is customary to hold a *Siyum Hasefer* upon the completion of a course of Jewish study.

Each year we finish reading our most important book, the Torah, and immediately begin reading it again. At this time we have a large celebration called *Simḥat Torah*. Traditionally, we have smaller celebrations when we finish studying other Jewish books. Such a celebration is called a *Siyum Hasefer*.

Include the students in the planning of the *Siyum Hasefer* so that they will feel that it is their celebration. Listed below are some appropriate activities that can be included:

- Invite the rabbi, cantor, education director, and parents.
- Recite the Sheheḥeyanu blessing.
- Serve refreshments accompanied by the appropriate blessings.
- Sing *Hatikvah* and other Hebrew songs.
- Play Hebrew team games.
- Present certificate of completion.

Make sure to create a lively, celebratory atmosphere in the classroom.

BLACK-LINE MASTERS

LESSON PLAN FORM

Teacher's Name _____ Grade _____ Lesson Date(s) _____

Text pages in *Shalom Uvrachah* to be covered _____

	Time Estimate
Instructional Materials Needed	

Goals:

Review

Introduce

Practice

Planned Activities

Homework Assigned

Notes

Dear Parent,

This year your child will acquire an exciting new skill—reading Hebrew. To make this as rewarding and successful an experience as possible, we need your help.

Once, not long ago, you taught your child a language. Your child was quite young and had no background in this language, but you had the ability and the patience to ensure success. You expressed your interest. You made clear your enthusiasm. And you were lavish in your praise.

We now call upon you to help us teach your child another language—Hebrew. Although you may not know Hebrew yourself, you can still contribute significantly. What is important is that you express your interest, praise your child's achievements, and motivate your child to learn.

Today the students received a new textbook called *Shalom Uvrachah* (Peace and Blessing). We hope you will take a few minutes to look through it. Your child can already read the first page. Why not ask your child to read this page to you? Let your child know that Hebrew studies are important to you. If you cannot read Hebrew and would like to learn, please let us know. We will be happy to make recommendations.

Learning to read Hebrew can be an adventure. We want you to encourage and share the excitement.

B'Shalom,

THE HEBREW ALPHABET

אבבגדההוז

חטיכככללמם

נןסעפפפףצץ

קרששתת

LESSONS

1–3

שׁ ת תּ בּ

ה כּ ל מ

־ ָ

Shalom Uvrachah, Behrman House, Inc.

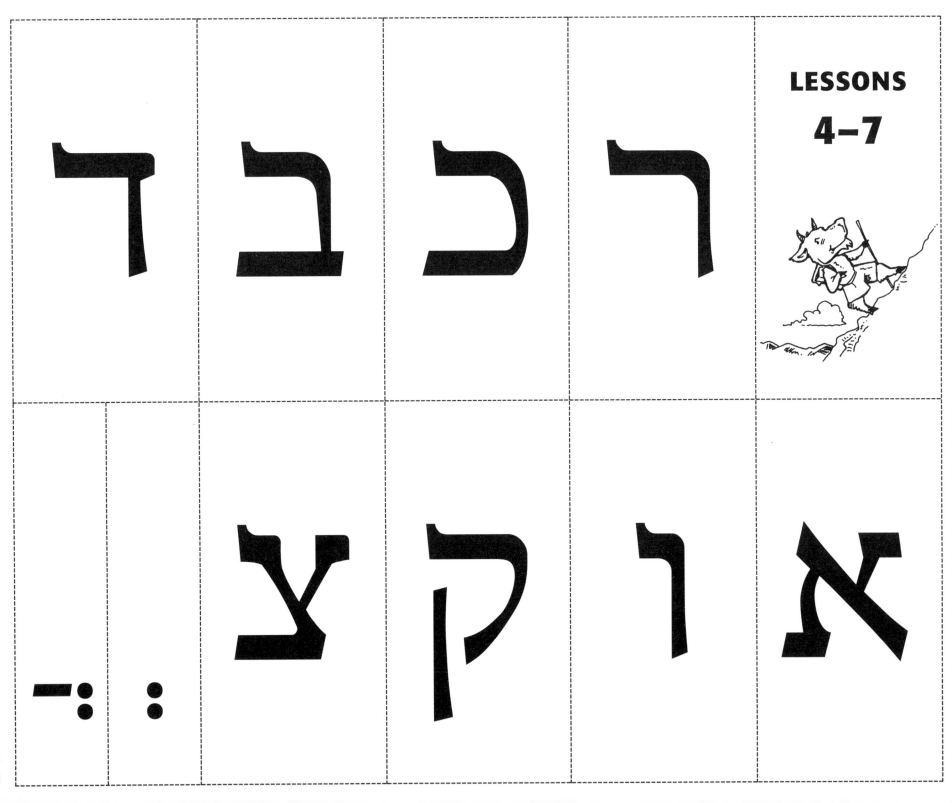

Shalom Uvrachah, Behrman House, Inc.

ד ב כ ב כ ר

ְ ֵ צ ק ו א

ח   ו   נ   ע

ל   ם   י   י

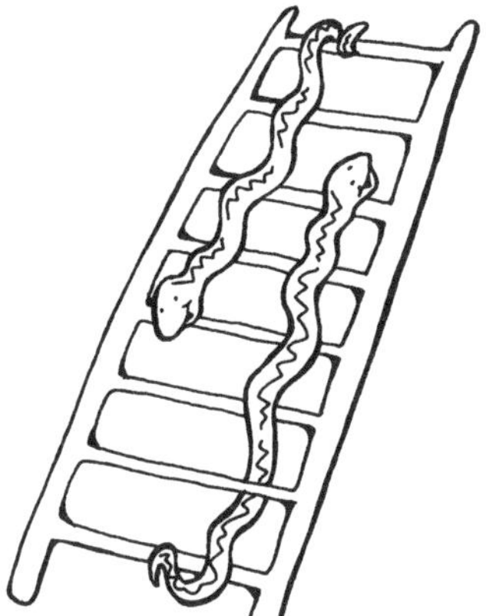

Shalom Uvrachah, Behrman House, Inc.

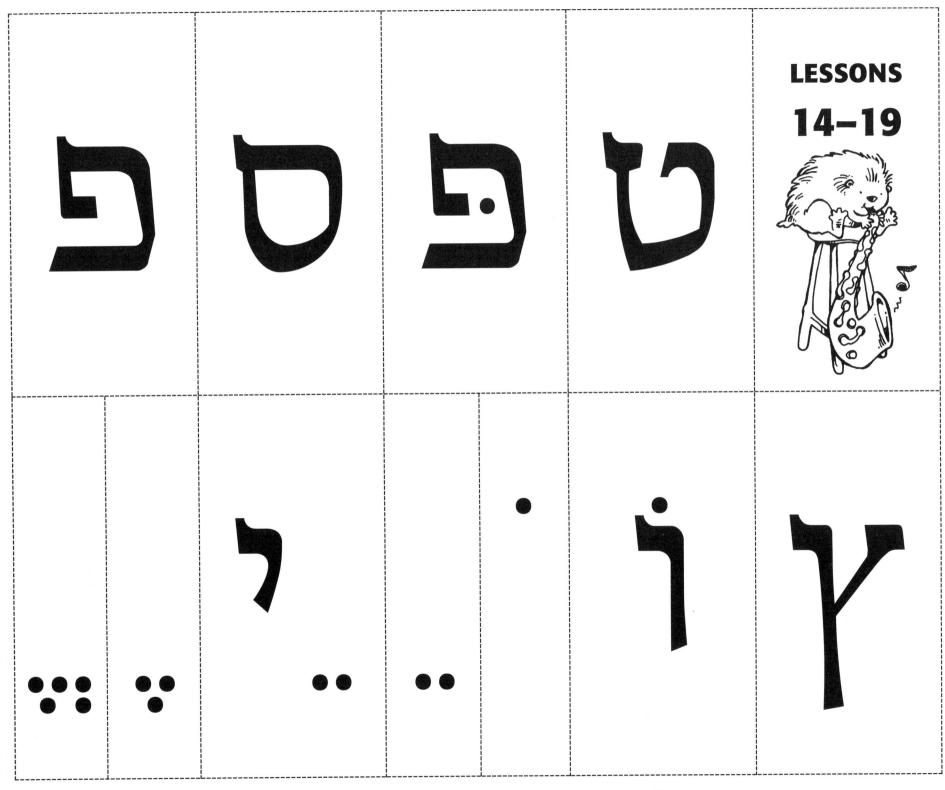

LESSONS 14–19

ט פ ס פ

ל

וֹ

ץ

ר

ז

ג

שׁ

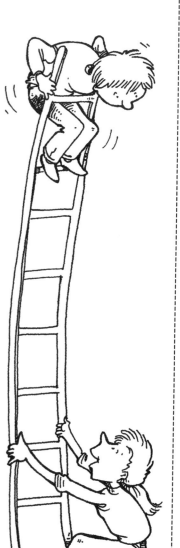

ק

וֹ

ִ

Shalom Uvrachah, Behrman House, Inc.

מַזָל טוֹב

_____

(Student's Name)

Has Completed the New Hebrew Primer

שָׁלוֹם וּבְרָכָה

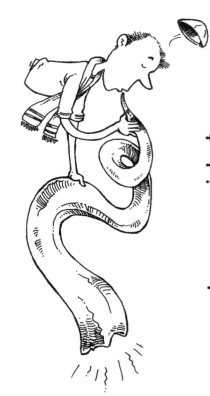

_____
Teacher

_____
Date

_____
Education Director

שָׁלוֹם וּבְרָכָה

THE NEW HEBREW PRIMER

Pearl Tarnor
Carol Levy

Activities:
Roberta Osser Baum

BEHRMAN HOUSE, INC.

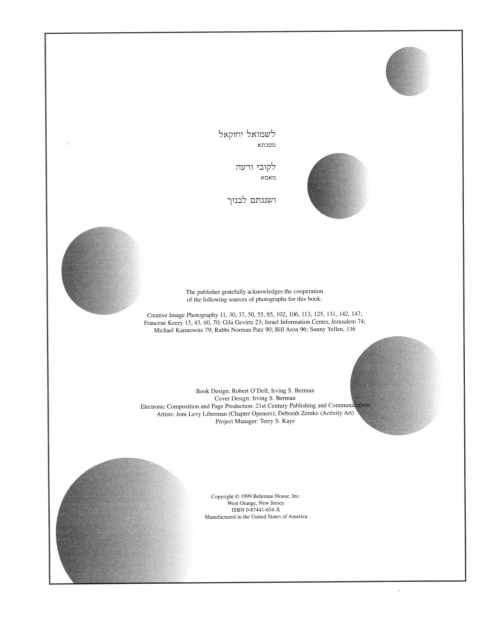

לשמואל יחזקאל
מסבתא

לקובי ורעה
מאמא

ושננתם לבניך

The publisher gratefully acknowledges the cooperation
of the following sources of photographs for this book:

Creative Image Photography 11, 30, 37, 50, 55, 85, 102, 106, 113, 125, 131, 142, 147;
Francene Keery 15, 43, 60, 70; Gila Gevirtz 23; Israel Information Center, Jerusalem 74;
Michael Kaimowitz 79; Rabbi Norman Patz 90; Bill Aron 96; Sunny Yellen, 136

Book Design: Robert O'Dell; Irving S. Berman
Cover Design: Irving S. Berman
Electronic Composition and Page Production: 21st Century Publishing and Communications
Artists: Joni Levy Liberman (Chapter Openers); Deborah Zemke (Activity Art)
Project Manager: Terry S. Kaye

TABLE OF CONTENTS

LESSON 1

Pages: 4–11
Key Word: שַׁבָּת
New Letters: ב ת ת שׁ
New Vowels: ָ ַ
Alef-Bet Flashcards: 1, 2, 3, 4, 5, 6
Word Cards: 1, 2

WELCOME TO HEBREW STUDY

Begin the class session by asking the students why the Hebrew language is important to the Jewish people. **[It is the language of the Jewish people. The Torah and many prayers are written in Hebrew.]**

KEY WORD – שַׁבָּת

What special things do we do on Shabbat? **[light candles, eat *ḥallah*, make Kiddush, eat special family meal together, go to services, etc.]** When do we use Hebrew on Shabbat? **[during services or when reciting prayers for home rituals mentioned above]**

Have the students create English sentences that include the word Shabbat and share them with the class.

Display and read word card #1 (שַׁבָּת) or write this word on the chalkboard.

INTRODUCING THE NEW LETTER – ב

Print a large *bet* on the chalkboard. Point to the letter *bet* on the chalkboard and on the word card and demonstrate its sound. Also point to the *bet* on the *alef-bet* chart posted in the room and have the students identify the letter's name and its sound.

INTRODUCING THE NEW VOWELS – (*KAMATZ*: ָ and *PATAḤ*: ַ)

Point to the *kamatz* and *pataḥ* on the *alef-bet* chart and demonstrate the sound that each vowel makes. Have the students repeat after you. Point to each vowel randomly and call upon a student to make its sound.

READING PRACTICE

Have the students open their textbooks and tell them to look at the letter and vowel in the middle of the Key word (שַׁבָּת). Also ask the students to identify the sounds **["b" and "ah"]** and the name of the letter **[bet]**.

Point again to the *bet* on the chalkboard and add a *pataḥ* or *kamatz* under it. Ask students to sound out the letter and then the vowel, each separately, and then to combine the sounds of the letter and the vowel.

Read line 1 for the class. (Make sure the students are following along.) Repeat the line in unison with the class. Continue this procedure with line 2. For lines 3 and 4, have each student read one "word" at a time.

SEARCH AND CIRCLE

Read each sound on line 1 and then ask students what is different about the circled sound. For the other three lines, read the sounds and have the students circle the one sound that is different. Then call on students to explain their answers.

SOUNDS LIKE

Read the instructions to the class and then have the students complete the exercise independently. When everyone has finished, call on students to read each line and explain their answers.

INTRODUCING THE NEW LETTER – ת ת

Display *alef-bet* flashcards #2 and #3 (ת ת) next to each other, or write both these letters on the chalkboard. Teach the name and sound of the *tav*. How do these two letters differ? **[presence of dot]** Emphasize that both letters are pronounced the same way.

Have the students point to the key word (שַׁבָּת) in the textbook. Read the word. Ask the students to point to the ת in שַׁבָּת. Does the *tav* in שַׁבָּת have a dot in it? **[no]**

READING PRACTICE

Call on students randomly to read these two lines aloud.

FYI

The *tav* without a *dagesh* (dot) used to be pronounced differently by the Ashkenazic Jewish communities of Eastern Europe. However, modern Hebrew has adopted the Sephardic pronunciation (emanating from Spanish and Middle-Eastern communities), in which both versions of the *tav*—with or without a *dagesh*—are identical.

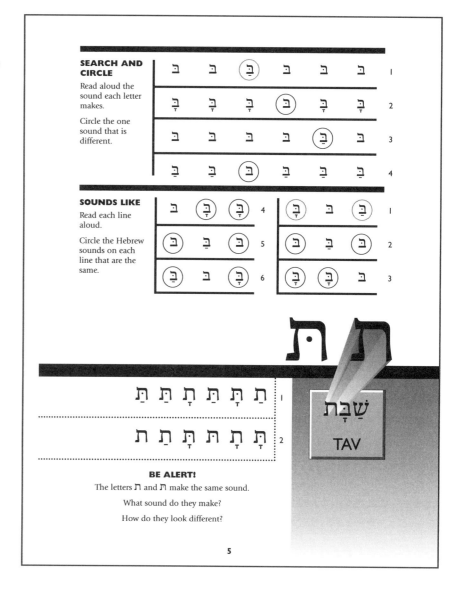

NOW READ & READ AGAIN

Have students take turns reading two words at a time with the class responding in unison.

HERITAGE WORD

Do you know a phrase that contains the word בַּת? [בַּת מִצְוָה]

What is a bat mitzvah? **[Literally means "daughter of the commandment." Becoming a bar or bat mitzvah means that according to Jewish tradition you are responsible for your own actions and it is now up to you to observe the *mitzvot*.]**

Have you attended a bar or bat mitzvah? What was it like?

WORD RIDDLE

Answer: תּוֹרָה

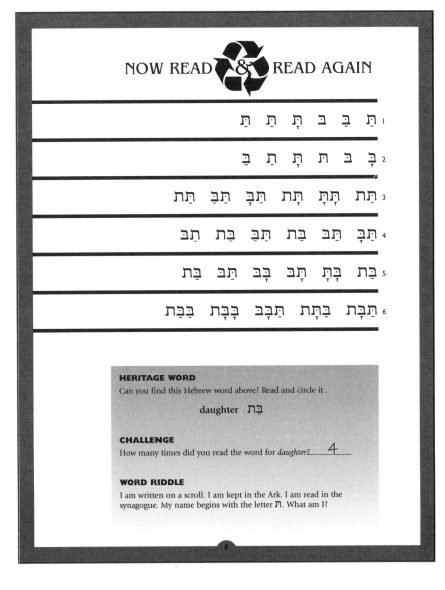

NOW READ & READ AGAIN

1 תַּ תָּ בַ תָ בַּ תַ

2 בָּ תַ תָ ת בַ בָּ

3 תַּת תַּבָ תָת תָּ תַּת

4 תַב בַּת תַּב בַּת תַּב תַּבָ

5 בַּת בַּב תָב בָּ בָּת בַּת

6 בַּבַת בָּבָ תַּבַב תָּת בַּתָּת תָּבָת

HERITAGE WORD
Can you find this Hebrew word above? Read and circle it .

daughter בַּת

CHALLENGE
How many times did you read the word for *daughter?* _4_

WORD RIDDLE
I am written on a scroll. I am kept in the Ark. I am read in the synagogue. My name begins with the letter ת. What am I?

6

SEARCH AND CIRCLE

Read each sound on line 1 and then ask the students what is different about the circled sound. For the other five lines, have the students complete the exercise independently. (The teacher should not read the sounds aloud.) Then call on students individually to identify the name and sound of the letter that differs from the others. Call on another student to identify the name and sound of the other matching letters on the line.

INTRODUCING THE NEW LETTER – שׁ

Print the letter *shin* on the chalkboard and teach its name and sound. Emphasize the location of the dot – on the top right of the *shin*. Have a student come to the *alef-bet* chart and point out the *shin*. Display word card #1 (שַׁבָּת) and have a student point out the *shin* in the word and read the word.

READING PRACTICE

Read lines 1 and 2 in unison. Then read line 3 to the class and call on students at random to repeat the line.

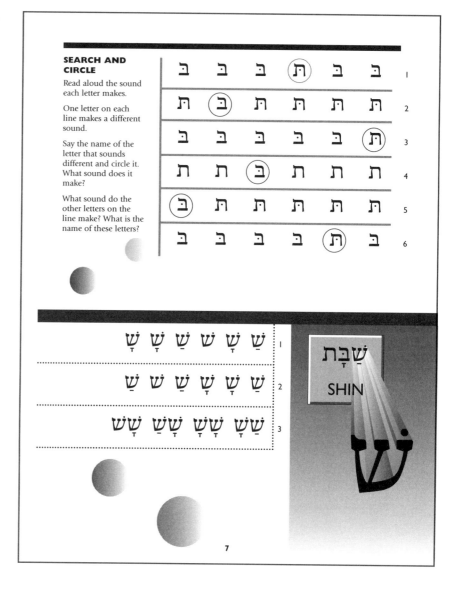

NOW READ & READ AGAIN

Call on students at random to read each of the lines. Keep students on their toes by sometimes calling on the same child more than once. Don't forget to recycle this section. Repeat it as many times as you find helpful.

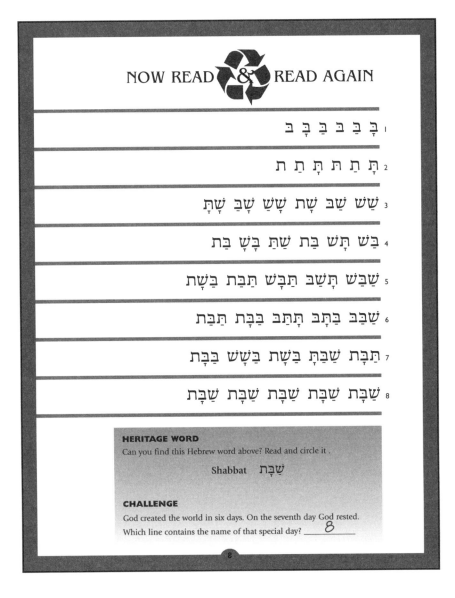

NOW READ & READ AGAIN

1. בָּ בַ בָ בַ בָּ בַ

2. תָ תַ ת תָ תַ ת

3. שֵׁשׁ שַׁב שָׁת שָׁשׁ שָׁב שָׁתּ

4. בֵּשׁ תָּשׁ בַּת שַׁתּ בָּשָׁ בַּת

5. שֵׁבַשׁ תָּשֵׁב תָּבָשׁ תַּבַּת בַּשָׁת

6. שֵׁבַּב בַּתָּב תָּתַּב בַּבָּת תַּבַּת

7. תַּבָת שַׁבַּתָ בַּשָׁת בַּשָּׁשׁ בַּבָּת

8. שַׁבָּת שַׁבַּת שַׁבָּת שַׁבָּת שַׁבָּת

HERITAGE WORD
Can you find this Hebrew word above? Read and circle it .

Shabbat   שַׁבָּת

CHALLENGE
God created the world in six days. On the seventh day God rested.
Which line contains the name of that special day? _____8_____

8

SEARCH AND CIRCLE/CONNECTIONS

Read the instructions and have the students complete these two exercises independently. Then have each pair up with a classmate to review their answers together.

If the students need additional practice in letter recognition, ask them to name all the letters in each row of the "Search and Circle" exercise.

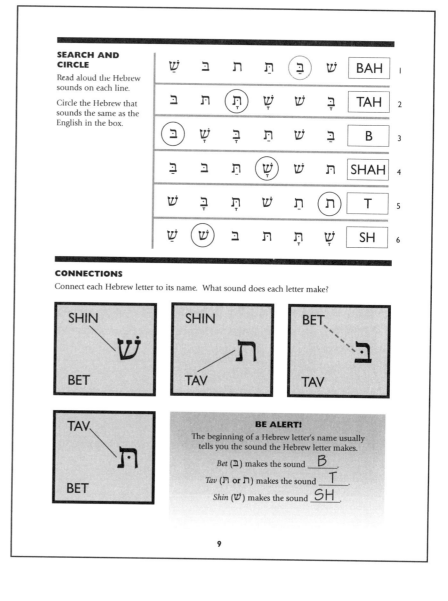

SEARCH AND CIRCLE

Read aloud the Hebrew sounds on each line.

Circle the Hebrew that sounds the same as the English in the box.

שַׁ	ב	תָּ	תַ	בַ	שׁ	BAH	1
ב	תָ	תַּ	שַּׁ	שׁ	בָ	TAH	2
בַ	שַׁ	בָ	תָ	שׁ	בַ	B	3
בָ	ב	תָ	שַׁ	שׁ	ת	SHAH	4
שׁ	בָ	תָ	שׁ	תַ	ת	T	5
שַׁ	שִׁ	ב	ת	תָ	שַׁ	SH	6

CONNECTIONS

Connect each Hebrew letter to its name. What sound does each letter make?

SHIN ש	SHIN ת	BET ב
BET	TAV	TAV

TAV ת	**BE ALERT!**
BET	The beginning of a Hebrew letter's name usually tells you the sound the Hebrew letter makes.

Bet (ב) makes the sound __B__.

Tav (ת or תּ) makes the sound __T__.

Shin (שׁ) makes the sound __SH__.

9

WRITING PRACTICE

Shalom Uvrachah [the student's edition] is available in two versions—one for teaching print writing and one for teaching script. This universal Teacher's Edition can be used with either version. You can see samples of every letter in script format on page xiv.

WRITE THE LETTERS

On the chalkboard, demonstrate the technique for writing the letter *bet*. Repeat it several times. Make sure that you are doing it slowly and that the students can see you forming the letter clearly. Have the students write the letter *bet* in the ruled lines provided in the textbook. Walk around the classroom and check to ensure that the students are writing the letter correctly. Make sure the students leave sufficient space between letters and words. Repeat this procedure with the *tav* and the *shin*.

WRITE THE WORDS

Write the word בַּת on the chalkboard. Then call on a few students to come to the chalkboard to write the word. All the students should then write the word בַּת in the space provided in the book. Repeat this procedure with the word שַׁבָּת.

FYI

Remember, this is the first time the students will be writing in Hebrew so offer plenty of encouragement! Remind them to look at the examples, which include guiding arrows, for assistance in how to form the letters properly.

WRITING PRACTICE

Write the Letters

בֵּ בֵּ בֵ בֵ

תָ תָ תָ תָ

שָׁ שָׁ שָׁ שָׁ

Write the Words

Write the Hebrew word for *daughter*.

בַּת בַּת

Write the Hebrew word for *Shabbat*.

שַׁבָּת שַׁבָּת

CIRCLE THE LETTERS

Circle the name of each letter.

Write each letter.

תּ	SHIN	(TAV)	BET	תּ	1
	(BET)	SHIN	TAV	בּ	2
	TAV	BET	(SHIN)	שׁ	3
	SHIN	BET	(TAV)	ת	4

10

USING THE PHOTOGRAPH

- Ask students to name the Shabbat objects on the dinner table.
  [Kiddush cups, wine, ḥallah and ḥallah cover, candles]
- What is the woman in the photograph doing? **[lighting Shabbat candles]**

WELCOMING SHABBAT

After the students have completed the exercise independently, ask them to name each of the objects in the exercise that we use to welcome Shabbat. **[ḥallah, wine cup, candlesticks]**

Also review the other objects not related to Shabbat and identify when they are used. **[gragger on Purim, lulav and etrog on Sukkot]**

Ask the students what they can do on Shabbat to make it a special day.

If there is time, discuss with the students why they think God commanded us to have a day of rest. **[God rested on the seventh day of creation; we all need rest so we can spend time with our family and friends; so we can appreciate our Jewishness; so we can enjoy the world that God created.]**

THE LIVING TRADITION שַׁבָּת

שַׁבָּת means "rest." We rest on the seventh day of the week. We call this day שַׁבָּת. On Friday evening, when שַׁבָּת begins, we welcome it with blessings and songs.

WELCOMING שַׁבָּת

Write the word שַׁבָּת on the line below each object we use to welcome שַׁבָּת.

11

LESSON 2

Pages: 12–15
Key Word: שַׁמָּשׁ
New Letter: מ
Alef-Bet Flashcard: 7
Word Card: 3

KEY WORD (שַׁמָּשׁ)

Draw a picture of a Ḥanukkah *menorah* on the chalkboard or bring one in to show to the class. Point to the candleholder that is higher up or otherwise differentiated from the others.

• What is this candle called? **[shamash]**
• What is the job of the *shamash*? **[to light the other candles]**
• How many other candles are there? **[8]**
• What other times do we use candles in Judaism? **[welcome Shabbat and holidays; part of *havdalah* ceremony to conclude Shabbat; *yahrtzeit* candle lit on anniversary of the death of a loved one]**
• Are there any other occasions when we use a *shamash*? **[no]**

INTRODUCING THE NEW LETTER – מ

Display word card #3 (שַׁמָּשׁ) or write the word on the chalkboard and have the students identify the vowels and letters they have already learned. [שׁ ָ] Point to the letter *mem* and teach its name and sound.

Take *alef-bet* flashcards #1–7 and hold them facing you. Turn around one card per student and have each student take a turn identifying the name and sound of the letter or vowel. After you have gone through the seven cards, shuffle them and repeat, so each child will have a turn with a new letter or vowel.

Display word card #3 again and have the students read the complete word.

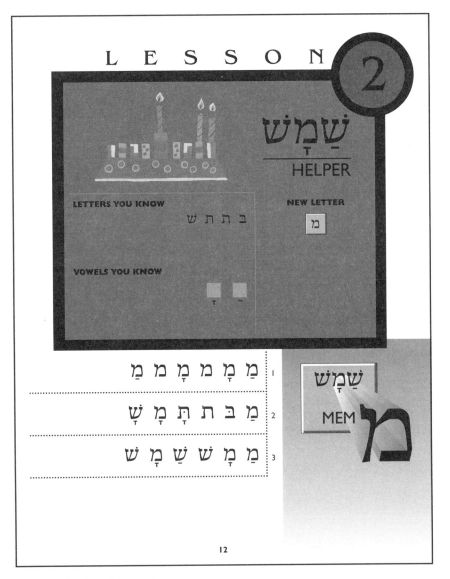

READING PRACTICE

Read line 1 for the class and have the students repeat the line in unison. Call on a student to read line 2 and then have the entire class repeat in unison. Repeat this procedure with line 3.

NOW READ & READ AGAIN

Call out a specific word, such as "line 3, fourth word" or "line 5, third word" and have a student read that word. Have the student call out the next word, or continue to call them out yourself.

HERITAGE WORD

Many synagogues used to have a person who was responsible for overseeing all the logistics of running the prayer services in the synagogue. This person was called the *shamas*. The *shamas* was someone who helped out in the synagogue. The word *shamas* actually comes from the Yiddish language but it has the same root as the word *shamash*.

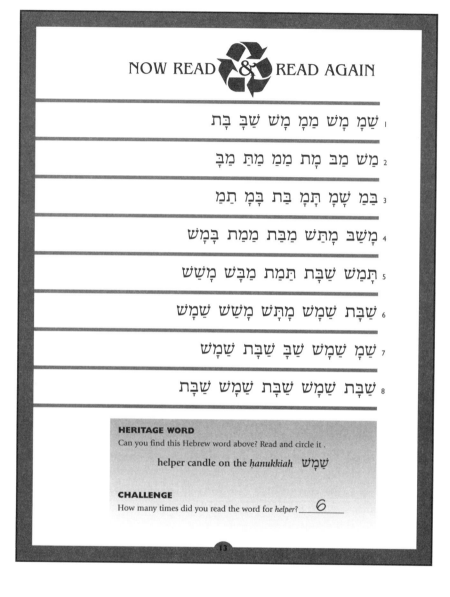

NOW READ & READ AGAIN

1. שֶׁמָ מָשׁ מַמָ מָשׁ שַׁבָ בָּת
2. מֶשׁ מַב מָת מֶם מַת מַבָ
3. בַּמ שָׁמָ תָּמָ בַּת בָּמָ תַּמ
4. מָשַׁב מָתֵשׁ מַבַת מַמַת בָּמָשׁ
5. תָּמַשׁ שַׁבָּת תַּמַת מַבָּשׁ מָשֵׁשׁ
6. שַׁבָּת שַׁמָשׁ מָתֵשׁ מָשֵׁשׁ שַׁמָשׁ
7. שַׁמָ שַׁמָשׁ שַׁבָ שַׁבָּת שַׁמָשׁ
8. שַׁבָּת שַׁמָשׁ שַׁבָּת שַׁמָשׁ שַׁבָּת

HERITAGE WORD

Can you find this Hebrew word above? Read and circle it.

helper candle on the *hanukkiah* שַׁמָשׁ

CHALLENGE

How many times did you read the word for *helper*? ___6___

13

SEARCH AND CIRCLE

Have the students complete this exercise independently. Then have them say the name and sound of the Hebrew letter in the box and identify the equivalent English sound.

WORD RIDDLE

Answer: מַצָּה

WRITING PRACTICE

Shalom Uvrachah [the student's edition] is available in two versions—one for teaching print writing and one for teaching script. This universal Teacher's Edition can be used with either version. You can see samples of every letter in script format on page xiv.

WRITE THE LETTER

On the chalkboard, demonstrate the technique for writing the letter *mem*. Have the students write the letter *mem* in the lines provided in the textbook. Walk around the classroom and check to ensure that the students are writing the letter correctly. Remind them that they can look at the example in the book if they forget the correct direction and sequence of lines.

WRITE THE WORDS

Write the word שֶׁמֶשׁ on the chalkboard. Then call on a few students to come to the chalkboard to write the word. All the students should then practice writing the word שֶׁמֶשׁ in the space provided in their book. Repeat this procedure for writing the word שַׁבָּת.

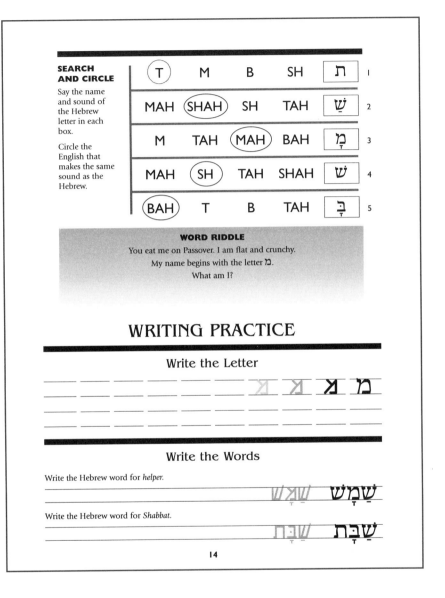

SEARCH AND CIRCLE

Say the name and sound of the Hebrew letter in each box.

Circle the English that makes the same sound as the Hebrew.

(T)	M	B	SH	ת	1
MAH	(SHAH)	SH	TAH	שָׁ	2
M	TAH	(MAH)	BAH	מָ	3
MAH	(SH)	TAH	SHAH	שֶׁ	4
(BAH)	T	B	TAH	בָּ	5

WORD RIDDLE

You eat me on Passover. I am flat and crunchy.
My name begins with the letter מ.
What am I?

WRITING PRACTICE

Write the Letter

Write the Words

Write the Hebrew word for *helper*.

שֶׁמֶשׁ

Write the Hebrew word for *Shabbat*.

שַׁבָּת

14

USING THE PHOTOGRAPH

- What night of Ḥanukkah is it? **[eighth]**
- How do you know? **[all eight candles are lit]**
- Which candle is the girl holding? **[shamash]**

HERITAGE CONNECTIONS

After students have completed the exercise independently, review the answers together aloud.

Go around the room and have the students quickly relate a happy memory connected with one of the pictures.

Another option is to divide the class into small groups and have them make up a short story that would include the words matzah, Torah, and Shabbat.

THE LIVING TRADITION שַׁמָּשׁ

שַׁמָּשׁ means "helper." The שַׁמָּשׁ is the helper candle on the *hanukkiah*, the Hanukkah *menorah*. We use the שַׁמָּשׁ to light the other candles.

HERITAGE CONNECTIONS

Connect each letter to the picture whose name begins with the same sound.

שׁ

מ

ת

NAME THE LETTER

Write the Hebrew letter under its name.

SHIN	BET	TAV	MEM
שׁ	בּ	תּ	מ

15

LESSON 3

Pages: 16–23
Key Word: כַּלָה
New Letters: ל כ ה
Alef-Bet Flashcards: 8, 9, 10
Word Cards: 4, 5

REVIEW EXERCISE

In this lesson your class will learn three new letters. Therefore, it is essential the students have a firm grasp of the letters and vowels that they already know.

Review the letters and vowels from the last two lessons by using a flannelboard or chalkboard. Set up the board with the letters. Point to each in turn as the students call out the sound. Have them respond first in unison and then individually.

KEY WORD (כַּלָה)

Have the students identify the picture at the top of the page. **[bride]**

Has anyone in the class attended a wedding? What was it like?

What things are unique to a Jewish wedding? [*ḥuppah* – **wedding canopy,** *ketubah* – **Jewish marriage contract, breaking the glass**]

Write the Key word – כַּלָה – on the chalkboard or display word card #4 and read the word to the class. Explain that all three letters that make up this word will be taught during this Lesson.

INTRODUCING THE NEW LETTER – ל

Introduce the new letter, *lamed*, by pointing it out in the word כַּלָה. Write a *lamed* on the chalkboard. Write a vowel under the *lamed* and have each student take a turn sounding out the new letter/vowel combination. Alternate the vowels.

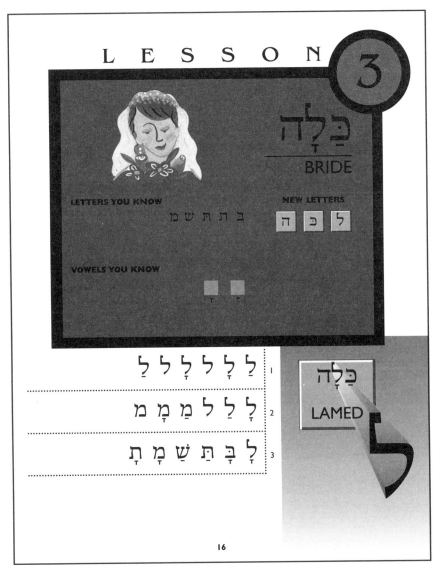

READING PRACTICE

Read the first line to the students and have them repeat the sounds in unison. Call on students to read line 2 and then have the class repeat in unison. Follow the same procedure for line 3.

NOW READ & READ AGAIN

Call on students to read a line of text aloud. As a change of pace, first have the students read all the odd-numbered lines followed by the even-numbered lines.

NOW READ & READ AGAIN

1 שַׁ שָׁ בַּ בָ תַּ תָ

2 תַּל שָׁל לָת לָשׁ מַמָ לָמָ

3 לַבַּ לָל לַת לָשָׁ לָמָ לֵת

4 מַל תַּל שָׁל בַּל לַל שָׁמָ

5 מַמָשׁ מַלָת בָּלַת שָׁלַשׁ בַּת

6 מָלַל לַבַּת תָּלַל מָשָׁל מָלַל

7 בַּלָשׁ שַׁמָשׁ תָּלַשׁ שָׁלָל לָמָשׁ

8 שֶׁמֶשׁ לַשֶּׁמֶשׁ שַׁבָּת לַשַׁבָּת שֶׁמֶשׁ

CHALLENGE

How many times did you read the Hebrew word for *helper*? __3__

Write the word. __שֶׁמֶשׁ__

How many times did you read the Hebrew word for *daughter*? __1__

Write the word. __בַּת__

17

SOUNDS LIKE

Read aloud the sounds on each line while the students complete the exercise according to the instructions.

INTRODUCING THE NEW LETTER – כ

Display *alef-bet* flashcard #1 (ב), or write it on the chalkboard, and have the class identify its name and sound. Then display *alef-bet* flashcard #9 (כ) and teach its name and sound. How do these two letters differ in appearance?

Have the students point to the *kaf* in the Key word in their textbooks.

READING PRACTICE

Read the first line to the students and have them repeat the sounds in unison. Call on students to read line 2 or 3, allowing each student the opportunity to choose the line. Have them identify the line number before reading.

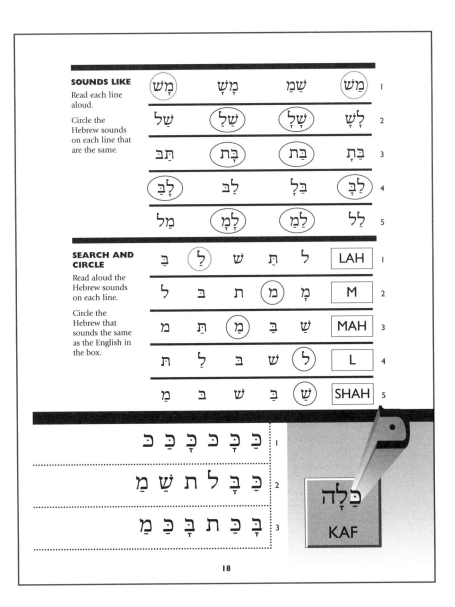

NOW READ & READ AGAIN

Number eight slips of paper 1 through 8 and put them in a small bag.
When it is each student's turn to read, the student picks a slip of paper
out of the bag and reads the line corresponding to the number on the
slip. Make sure to recycle the exercise in order to provide reading
practice to as many students as possible.

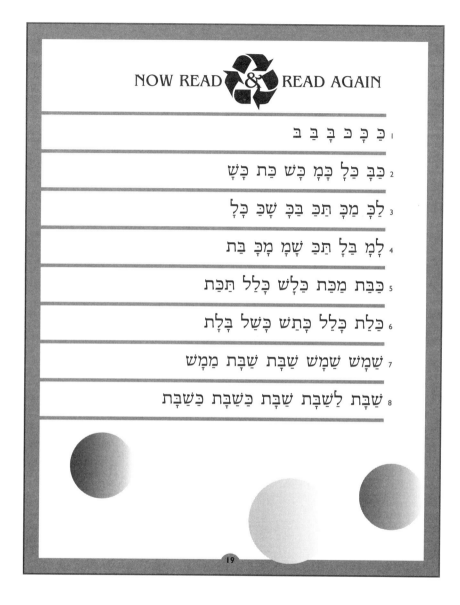

NOW READ & READ AGAIN

1. בַּ בָּ בְּ כַ כָ כְּ

2. כַּב כַּל כָּמְ כָּשׁ כַּת כָּשָׁ

3. לַךְ מַךְ תַּכ בַּךְ שָׁכַּ כָּל

4. לָמְ בַּל תַּכ שָׁמְ מָךְ בַת

5. כַּבַּת מַכַּת כַּלָשׁ כָּלַל תַּכַּת

6. כַּלַת כָּלַל כָּתַשׁ כָּשַׁל בָּלַת

7. שַׁמְשׁ שַׁמְשׁ שַׁבָּת שַׁבָּת מַמְשׁ

8. שַׁבָּת לַשַׁבָּת שַׁבָּת כַּשַׁבָּת כַּשַׁבָּת

19

SOUND OFF

Have the students complete the exercise independently, and then call on individual students to say the name of the Hebrew letter and its sound.

INTRODUCE THE NEW LETTER – ה

Point to the *hay* on the *alef-bet* chart and teach its name and sound. Make sure to read and explain the "Be Alert" section.

READING PRACTICE

Have the students look at the Key word כַּלָה and identify the name and sound of each letter. Have the students read the key word and define it.

• Does the *hay* have the "h" sound in this word? **[no]**
• Why not? **[It is the final letter in the word and it has no vowel connected to it]**

Call on students at random to read one of the three lines.

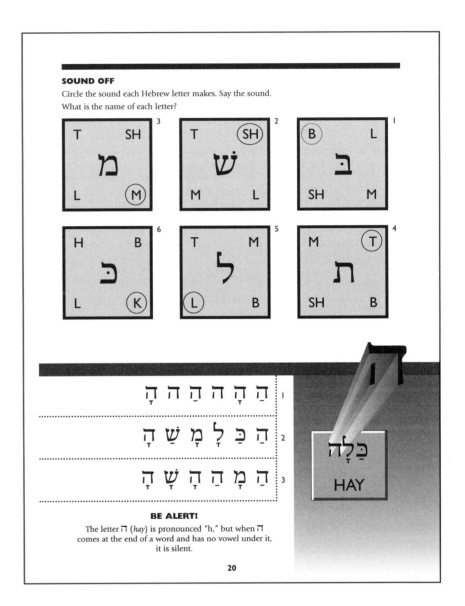

SOUND OFF

Circle the sound each Hebrew letter makes. Say the sound. What is the name of each letter?

BE ALERT!

The letter ה (*hay*) is pronounced "h," but when ה comes at the end of a word and has no vowel under it, it is silent.

20

NOW READ & READ AGAIN

Have students read three words at a time. The first student reads three words. The second student overlaps by reading three words beginning with the second word. The third student begins with the third word, and so on.

HERITAGE WORDS

At Shabbat services on Friday night we sing *L'cha Dodi Likrat Kallah.* Does anyone recognize this song? Can anyone sing the song or hum the tune?

This song compares Shabbat to a bride, and when we sing it we welcome the Shabbat bride.
• What words can be used to describe a bride on her wedding day?
[happy, glowing, nervous, excited, beautiful, etc.]

At the end of this Lesson you will discuss why it might be appropriate to compare Shabbat to a bride.

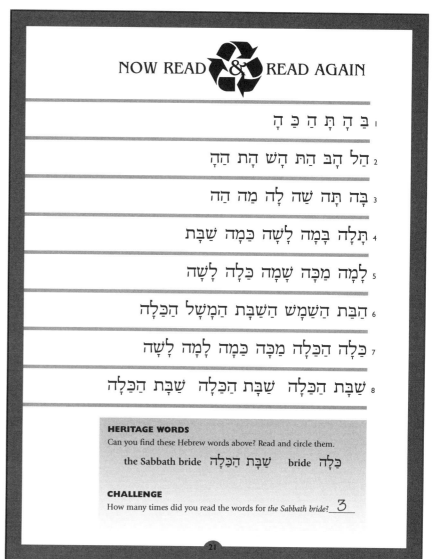

NOW READ & READ AGAIN

1 בַּ הָ תָּ הַ כָ הָ

2 הַל הָב הַת הַת הָשׁ הָת הַהּ

3 בָּה תָּה שַׁה לָה מַה הַה

4 תָּלָה בָּמָה לָשָׁה כַּמָה שַׁבָּת

5 לָמָה מַכָּה שָׁמָה כַּלָה לָשָׁה

6 הַבַּת הַשָּׁמָשׁ הַשַּׁבָּת הַמָשָׁל הַכַּלָה

7 כַּלָה הַכַּלָה מַכָּה כַּמָה לָמָה לָשָׁה

8 שַׁבָּת הַכַּלָה   שַׁבָּת הַכַּלָה   שַׁבָּת הַכַּלָה

HERITAGE WORDS
Can you find these Hebrew words above? Read and circle them.
the Sabbath bride   שַׁבָּת הַכַּלָה   bride כַּלָה

CHALLENGE
How many times did you read the words for *the Sabbath bride?* _3_

21

WRITING PRACTICE

Shalom Uvrachah [the student's edition] is available in two versions—one for teaching print writing and one for teaching script. This universal Teacher's Edition can be used with either version. You can see samples of every letter in script format on page xiv.

WRITE THE LETTERS

On the chalkboard, demonstrate the technique for writing the letter *lamed*. Repeat it several times. Have the students write the letter *lamed* in the lines provided in the textbook. Ensure that the students realize that part of the *lamed* is written <u>above</u> the ruled line. Repeat this procedure with the *kaf* and the *hay*.

SEARCH AND CIRCLE

Read the instructions and have the students complete this exercise independently. Then call on students to say the name and sound of the Hebrew letter in the box and identify the equivalent English sound.

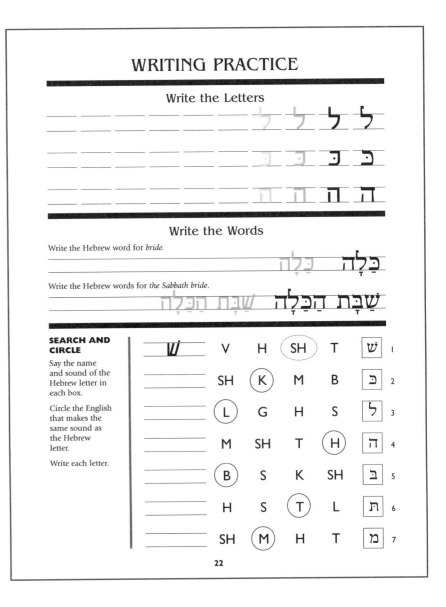

USING THE PHOTOGRAPH

How do you know the woman in the photograph is a *kallah*? **[she is wearing a veil]**

THE LIVING TRADITION

Discuss the question asked in the book, "Why do you think Shabbat is compared to a *kallah*?" **[Shabbat is the loving companion to the Jewish people.]** The following questions will help the students to come up with an answer:

• Who else is at a wedding? **[family, friends, rabbi, etc.]**
• If Shabbat is the bride, who is the groom? **[the Jewish people]**
• Who is the rabbi? **[God]**

To help the students answer the question, you might also ask them to compare how they might feel at a wedding and how they feel on Shabbat. **[excitement, anticipation, etc.]**

AN *ALEF-BET* CHART

Encourage the students to be creative in coloring in the letters on their personal *alef-bet* chart, which can be found on page 160. Use different colors, designs, etc. While the students are coloring, you might play some modern Israeli music in the background to demonstrate to the students that Hebrew is a modern, living language and not exclusively used for ritual purposes.

THE LIVING TRADITION כַּלָּה

Every Friday evening as we welcome שַׁבָּת, we say that שַׁבָּת is like a bride—כַּלָּה. Just as a כַּלָּה is joyously welcomed at the wedding ceremony, so we welcome שַׁבָּת with great happiness.

Why do you think שַׁבָּת is compared to a כַּלָּה?

WORD MATCH

Draw a line to match each Hebrew term with its English meaning.
Read each Hebrew-English match aloud.

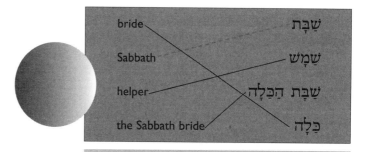

bride
Sabbath
helper
the Sabbath bride

שַׁבָּת
שֶׁמֶשׁ
שַׁבָּת הַכַּלָּה
כַּלָּה

AN *ALEF BET* CHART

You know these Hebrew letters:

ב ת ת שׁ מ ל ה כ

Turn to the *Alef Bet* Chart on page 160.

Color in the letters you have learned. You will return to the chart again after a few more lessons. The more letters you learn, the more colorful the *Alef Bet* Chart will become.

23

LESSON THREE

23

LESSON 4

Pages: 24–30
Key Word: בְּרָכָה
New Letters: כ ר
New Vowel: ְ
Alef-Bet Flashcards: 11, 12, 13
Word Cards: 6, 7, 8

REVIEW EXERCISE

I Spy

Play the "I Spy" game described in #7 on page viii. Use flashcards #1–10.

This game can be modified by writing the letters and vowels on the chalkboard.

KEY WORD (בְּרָכָה)

What is the first word is in almost every blessing we recite? **[baruch]**
What is the Hebrew word for blessing? **[בְּרָכָה]**

Have the students list different *brachot* that they are familiar with. They will probably be surprised at how many they already know!

Have the students look at the Key word in the textbook and ask them to identify the names and sounds of the letters and vowels that they know. **[bet, hay, and kamatz – ָ]**

INTRODUCE THE NEW LETTER – ר

Announce "I spy a *resh*!" and point to the *resh* on the *alef-bet* chart. Ask the students to guess the sound that the *resh* makes.

INTRODUCE THE NEW VOWEL – (SHVAH: ְ)

Write a *shvah* on the chalkboard and ask if any of the students can "spy" it on the *alef-bet* chart. Take flashcards #5, 6, and 13 (the three vowels learned to this point) and drill the students on the vowel sounds.

READING PRACTICE

Randomly call on students to read each of these three lines. Remember, these lines can be repeated to give more students a chance to read.

NOW READ & READ AGAIN

Have one student read a line and then call out another line number for the next student to read. The same line should not be read consecutively.

HERITAGE WORDS

What are the names of the two queens who are part of the story of Purim? **[Vashti and Esther]**

Shabbat is sometimes compared to what two types of women?
[שַׁבָּת הַמַלְכָּה – Shabbat Queen, שַׁבָּת הַכַּלָה – Shabbat Bride]

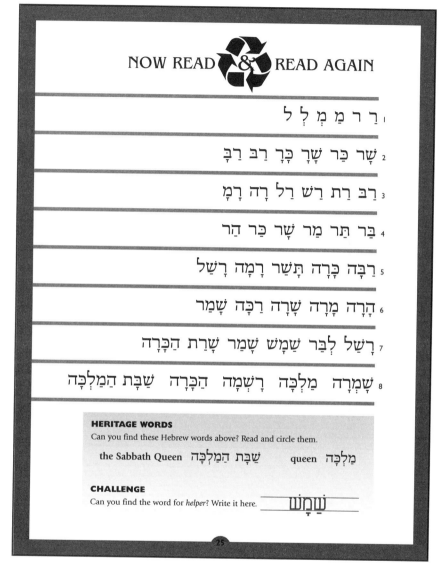

NOW READ & READ AGAIN

1 רַ ר רַ מַ מְ לֵ לֹ

2 שָׁר כַּר שָׁךְ כָּךְ רַב רַבְּ

3 רַב רַת רַשׁ רַל רָה רָמָ

4 בַּר תַּר מַר שָׁר כַּר הַר

5 רַבָּה כָּרָה תָּשַׁר רָמָה רָשַׁל

6 הָרָה מָרָה שָׁרָה רַכָּה שָׁמַר

7 רָשַׁל לְבַר שֶׁמֶשׁ שָׁמַר שָׁרַת הַכָּרָה

8 שָׁמְרָה מַלְכָּה רָשְׁמָה הַכָּרָה שַׁבָּת הַמַלְכָּה

HERITAGE WORDS
Can you find these Hebrew words above? Read and circle them.

the Sabbath Queen שַׁבָּת הַמַלְכָּה   queen מַלְכָּה

CHALLENGE
Can you find the word for *helper*? Write it here. ___שֶׁמֶשׁ___

25

NAME TAG

Have the students complete the exercise independently. When you are reviewing the answers together, after a student gives the correct answer have the student get up and "tag" a classmate to answer the next line.

INTRODUCE THE NEW LETTER – כ

Display *alef-bet* flashcard # 9 (ב) and have the students identify its name and the sound it makes. Hold *alef-bet* flashcard #12 (כ) next to it and ask the students how the two differ in appearance. Teach the name and sound of the *chaf*. This can also be done by displaying these letters on a flannelboard.

The "*ch*" sound may be difficult for some students since there is no equivalent sound in English. You may want to compare it to the expression some people make regarding a food or something else which disgusts them – "*yuch*." Be diligent in encouraging the students to pronounce the "*ch*" sound since some will lazily pronounce it "*k*."

READING PRACTICE

Read line 1 for the class and have the class repeat the line in unison. Call on a student to read line 2 and then have the entire class repeat in unison. Repeat this procedure with line 3.

Have the students read the Key word – בְּרָכָה

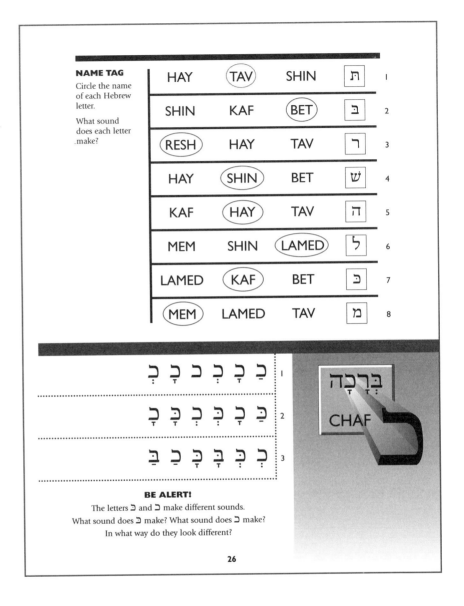

NAME TAG
Circle the name of each Hebrew letter.

What sound does each letter make?

HAY	(TAV)	SHIN	ת	1
SHIN	KAF	(BET)	ב	2
(RESH)	HAY	TAV	ר	3
HAY	(SHIN)	BET	שׁ	4
KAF	(HAY)	TAV	ה	5
MEM	SHIN	(LAMED)	ל	6
LAMED	(KAF)	BET	כ	7
(MEM)	LAMED	TAV	מ	8

בְּ כָ כְ כָ כִ 1
כָ כְ כָ כִ כֵ 2
כְ כִ כָ כֵ בַּ 3

בְּרָכָה
CHAF כ

BE ALERT!
The letters ב and כ make different sounds.
What sound does ב make? What sound does כ make?
In what way do they look different?

26

NOW READ & READ AGAIN

Have a student read until you clap your hands. At that time, the next student reads. Determine the number of words according to the student's ability and reading fluency, keeping the pace lively. Students who can read faster may read more words and slower students may read fewer words in this exercise. Don't forget to recycle the reading exercise.

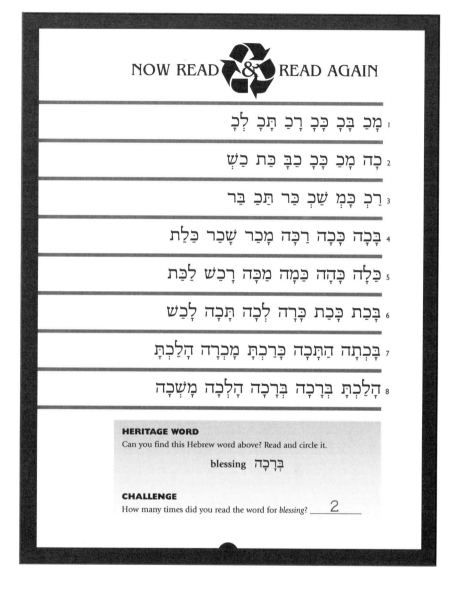

NOW READ & READ AGAIN

1 מְכַ בְּכַ כָּכַ רְכַ תְּכַ לְכָ

2 כָה מְכַ כְּכָ כַבְּ כַּת כַשׁ

3 רַכְ כָּמְ שַׂכְ כַּר תַּכַ בַּר

4 בְּכָה כָּכָה רַכָּה מָכַר שָׂכַר כַּלַּת

5 כַּלָה כָּהָה כְּמָה מַכָּה רְכַשׁ לַכַּת

6 בָּכַת כָּכַת כָּרָה לְכָה תְּכָה לָכַשׁ

7 בָּכְתָה הַתְּכָה כָּרַכְתָּ מִכְרָה הָלַכְתָּ

8 הָלַכְתָּ בְּרָכָה בְּרָכָה הָלְכָה מָשְׁכָה

HERITAGE WORD
Can you find this Hebrew word above? Read and circle it.

blessing בְּרָכָה

CHALLENGE
How many times did you read the word for *blessing*? ___2___

RHYME TIME

Call on students to read the words in both columns aloud. Then go through the words one by one, having the students identify each rhyming set. Keep in mind that sometimes there may be other rhyming combinations, but each word has a "partner" which is its best match.

SEARCH AND CIRCLE

Have the students complete this exercise independently. Then call on them to identify the name and sound of the letter that doesn't belong, followed by the name and sound of the other letters on each line.

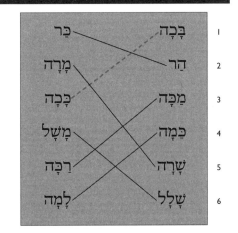

RHYME TIME

Read aloud the Hebrew words in each column.

Connect the rhyming words. Read the rhyming sets aloud.

בְּכָה	כַּר	1
הַר	מָרָה	2
מַכָּה	כָּכָה	3
כַּמָּה	מָשָׁל	4
שָׂרָה	רַכָּה	5
שָׁלָל	לָמָה	6

SEARCH AND CIRCLE

Read aloud the sound each letter makes.

One letter on each line makes a different sound.

Say the name of the letter that sounds different and circle it. What sound does it make?

What sound do the other letters on the line make? What is the name of that letter?

בּ	בּ	בּ	(ת)	בּ	בּ	בּ	1
כּ	(בּ)	כּ	כּ	כּ	כּ	כּ	2
(ה)	ת	ת	ת	ת	ת	ת	3
כ	כ	כ	כ	כ	(ת)	כ	4
ה	ה	ה	ה	(ר)	ה	ה	5
כ	כ	כ	(כּ)	כ	כ	כ	6

28

WRITING PRACTICE

Don't forget that *Shalom Uvrachah* [the student's edition] is available in two versions—one for teaching print writing and one for teaching script. This universal Teacher's Edition can be used with either version. You can see samples of every letter in script format on page xiv.

ODD ONE OUT

Have several students at a time come to the chalkboard with their books, copy the letters from a given line, and circle the appropriate letter. Continue in the same manner until the exercise has been completed. The rest of the students should complete the exercise in their books.

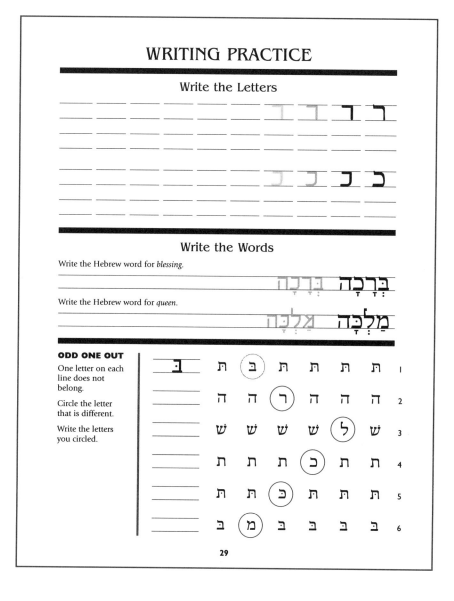

USING THE PHOTOGRAPH

What is the family in the photograph doing? **[lighting candles for Shabbat or a holiday]**

Recite the *brachah* over the Shabbat candles together.

בָּרוּךְ אַתָּה ה׳ אֱלֹהֵינוּ מֶלֶךְ הָעוֹלָם, אֲשֶׁר קִדְּשָׁנוּ בְּמִצְוֹתָיו
וְצִוָּנוּ לְהַדְלִיק נֵר שֶׁל שַׁבָּת.

THE LIVING TRADITION

Ask the question found in the book, "What do you thank God for?" List all the different answers on the chalkboard.

As the students learned at the beginning of the lesson when they listed all the *brachot* they knew, there are *brachot* for many different occasions. Teach them that if they want to thank God for something but they don't know the appropriate *brachah*, they can always say the following general *brachah*. This teaches that there is truly a *brachah* for every occasion and that everything in life affords us an opportunity to consider God.

בָּרוּךְ אַתָּה ה׳ אֱלֹהֵינוּ מֶלֶךְ הָעוֹלָם הַטּוֹב וְהַמֵּטִיב.

Praised are You, Adonai our God, Ruler of the universe, who is good and does good things.

WORD MATCH

Read the instructions and have the students complete the exercise independently.

CHALLENGE

Read the instructions and then go around the room having the students say their sentences.

THE LIVING TRADITION בְּרָכָה

A בְּרָכָה is a blessing. When we say a בְּרָכָה we thank God for the gifts God gives us. For example, we thank God for the food we eat, for the Shabbat wine we drink, and even for a rainbow that stretches across the sky.

What do you thank God for?

WORD MATCH

Read the Hebrew words in the box.
Write each Hebrew word next to its English meaning.

שַׁבָּת שֶׁמֶשׁ כַּלָּה בְּרָכָה מַלְכָּה

1 helper   שֶׁמֶשׁ

2 queen   מַלְכָּה

3 bride   כַּלָּה

4 Shabbat   שַׁבָּת

5 blessing   בְּרָכָה

CHALLENGE

Can you use each Hebrew word in an English sentence?
Example: We welcome שַׁבָּת by lighting candles.

30

LESSON 5

Pages: 31–37
Key Word: הַבְדָלָה
New Letters: ב ד
New Vowel: ֲ
Alef-Bet Flashcards: 14, 15, 16
Word Card: 9

REVIEW EXERCISE

Baseball

Play the "Baseball" game described in #5 on page viii. Use flashcards #1–13

Before the students tire of the game, take a "timeout" to introduce the new Key word, letter, and vowel. After the new letter and vowel are taught, return to the game, adding flashcards #14 and #16.

KEY WORD (הַבְדָלָה)

Display word card #1 (שַׁבָּת), or write the word on the chalkboard, and have the students read and define the word. Then ask the students to name the ceremony we recite on Saturday night at the end of Shabbat.

Explain that the word *havdalah* literally means "separation." Why do the students think we use *havdalah* as the name for this ceremony? **[It separates the holiness and specialness of Shabbat from the ordinary nature of the rest of the week.]** What objects do we use during the *havdalah* ceremony? **[spice box, Kiddush cup, braided candle]**

INTRODUCE THE NEW LETTER – ב

Have the students look at the Key word in the textbook or display word card #9. Which letters do they recognize? **[bay, lamed]** What does the second letter in the word resemble? **[bet]** How is it different? **[no dot]** Hold up *alef-bet* flashcard #1 (בּ) next to flashcard #14 (ב). Pronounce clearly the difference in sounds.

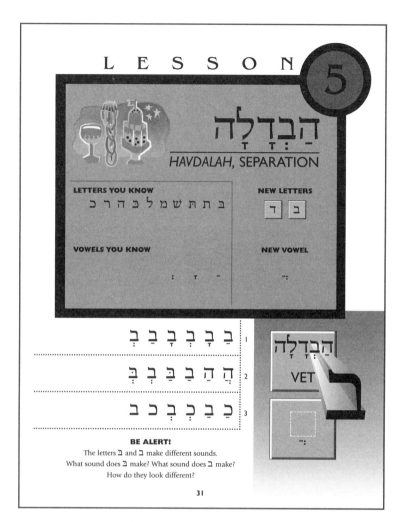

INTRODUCE THE NEW VOWEL – (*HATAF PATAH*: ֲ)

Hold up flashcard #16 (ֲ) Ask the class what two vowels they recognize. Explain that this vowel is sounded the same as the *patah*.

READING PRACTICE

Continuing the use of the "baseball theme," call on individuals to read each of the three lines and then have their teammates repeat in unison.

NOW READ & READ AGAIN

Draw a tic-tac-toe grid on the chalkboard. Divide the class into two teams. To place an X or an O on the board, the students must correctly read a line, or word, in the book.

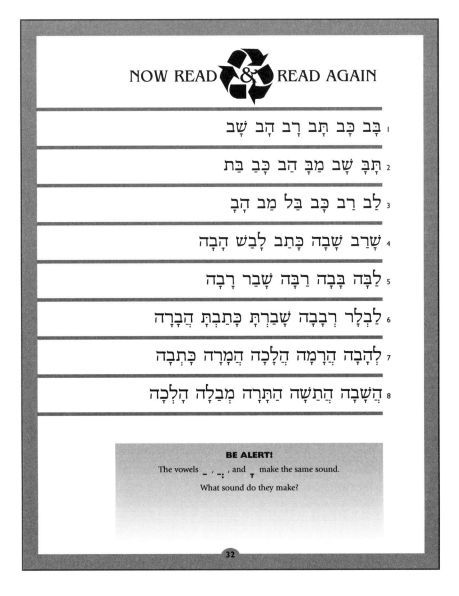

NOW READ & READ AGAIN

1 בָּב כָּב תָּב רָב הָב שָׁב

2 תָּבְ שָׁב מַבְּ הַב כָּבַ בַּת

3 לַב רַב כָּב בֵּל מַב הָב

4 שָׂרֵב שָׁבָה כָּתַב לָבַשׁ הָבָה

5 לַבָּה בָּבָה רַבָּה שָׁבַר רְבָה

6 לִבְלֵר רְבְבָה שָׁבַרְתָּ כָּתַבְתָּ הַבְרָה

7 לְהָבָה הֲרָמָה הֲלָכָה הַמָּרָה כָּתְבָה

8 הֲשָׁבָה הַתַּשָׁה הַתָּרָה מְבַלָּה הָלְכָה

BE ALERT!
The vowels ָ , ֳ , and ָ make the same sound.
What sound do they make?

32

WORD WIZARD

After the students have completed this exercise, write each of the Key words from the first four lessons on the chalkboard:

בְּרָכָה   כַּלָּה   שֶׁמֶשׁ   שַׁבָּת

Have the students define them, and then have the students choose one to embed in their own Word Wizard, as was done in the exercise with the word בְּרָכָה. Then have the students exchange their work and complete the exercise.

INTRODUCE THE NEW LETTER – ד

Point to the *resh* on the *alef-bet* chart and have the students identify its name and the sound it makes. Then point to the *dalet* and teach its name and sound. How do these two letters differ in appearance? A helpful hint to the students is always to remember that "*resh* is rounded."

Display word card #9 or write the Key word on the chalkboard, and have the students point out the *dalet* in the word and then read the word.

READING PRACTICE

As a change of pace, tell the students to read the sounds on the three lines vertically. This variation will provide six columns of three words each.

WORD WIZARD

Discover a hidden word.

Cross out the Hebrew letters and their vowels that match the English sounds below.

Write the remaining Hebrew letters and their vowels on the lines below to discover the hidden word.

1 SHAH	4 HAH
2 V	5 K
3 LAH	6 T

What does the word mean? _____ *blessing*

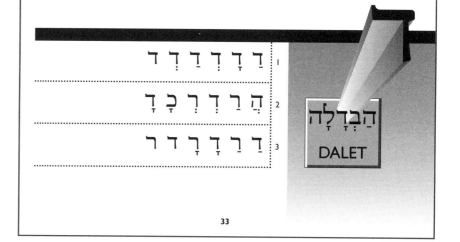

NOW READ & READ AGAIN

Call on students at random to read each of the lines. Keep students on their toes by calling on the same child more than once.

HERITAGE WORD

An additional question to ask is, "What other word(s) that you have learned appear above?" [בְּרָכָה] If the students cannot figure it out, give them the hint to look in line 8.

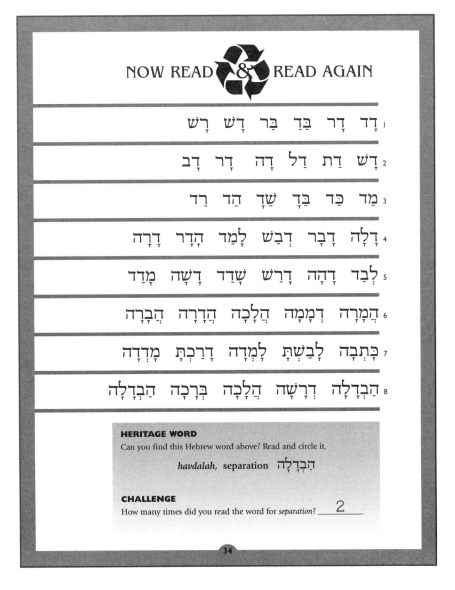

NOW READ & READ AGAIN

1 דָּד דָּר בַּד בַּר דָּשׁ רָשׁ

2 דָּשׁ דַּת דַּל דָּה דָּר דָּב

3 מַד כַּד בַּדְ שַׁדְ הַד רַד

4 דְּלָה דָּבָר דְּבַשׁ לָמַד הָדָר דָּרָה

5 לְבַד דָּהָה דָּרַשׁ שַׁדַּד דָּשָׁה מָדַד

6 הֶמְרָה דְּמָמָה הֲלָכָה הֲדָרָה הַבְרָה

7 כְּתָבָה לָבַשְׁתָּ לָמְדָה דָּרַכְתָּ מָדְדָה

8 הַבְדָּלָה דְּרָשָׁה הֲלָכָה בְּרָכָה הַבְדָּלָה

HERITAGE WORD

Can you find this Hebrew word above? Read and circle it.

havdalah, **separation** הַבְדָּלָה

CHALLENGE

How many times did you read the word for *separation*? __2__

34

SOUNDS LIKE/SEARCH AND CIRCLE

Have the students complete these exercises independently, and then call on students to read each line and provide the answer.

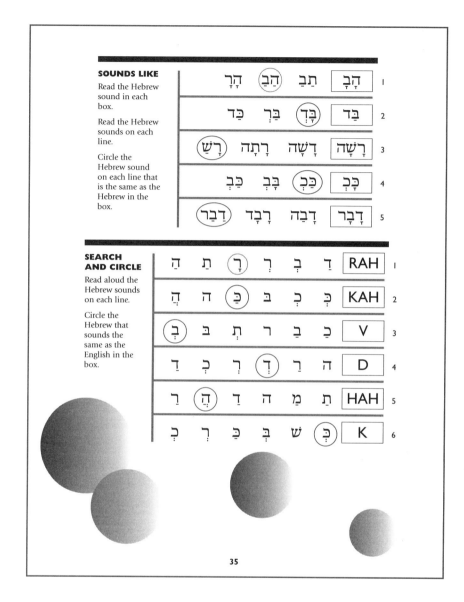

SOUNDS LIKE

Read the Hebrew sound in each box.

Read the Hebrew sounds on each line.

Circle the Hebrew sound on each line that is the same as the Hebrew in the box.

1. הָב | תַב | הַב | הָר
2. בַּד | כַּד | בַּר | בְּד
3. רֵשׁ | דָשָׁה | רָתָה | רֵשׁ
4. כָּכ | כַּב | בְּב | כָּכ
5. דְבָר | דָבַר | רָבָד | דָבַה

SEARCH AND CIRCLE

Read aloud the Hebrew sounds on each line.

Circle the Hebrew that sounds the same as the English in the box.

1. RAH | הַ | תַ | דַ | בְּ | רְ | רָ | הָ
2. KAH | הָ | כַּ | ה | ב | כְ | כֵ | כָ
3. V | בְ | תָ | ר | ב | כַ | בְּ
4. D | דַ | כְ | רְ | דְ | ר | הַ
5. HAH | רְ | הָ | ד | ה | מַ | תַ | ר
6. K | כֵ | רְ | בְּ | שׁ | כֵ | כְ

35

LESSON FIVE

35

WRITE THE LETTERS

Ask for a volunteer to come to the chalkboard and demonstrate the technique for writing the letter *bet*. Explain that the *vet* is written the same way, except without the dot (*dagesh*). Have the students write the letter *vet* in the ruled lines provided in the textbook.

On the chalkboard, demonstrate the technique for writing the letter *dalet*. Repeat it several times. Have the students write the letter *dalet* in the ruled lines provided in the textbook. Walk around the room and ensure that the students are writing the *dalet* correctly, and if you are teaching print writing that they are not writing it like a *resh*.

NAME TAG

Read aloud the name of the Hebrew letter in each box and have the students circle the matching Hebrew letter on that line and then write the letter in the space provided.

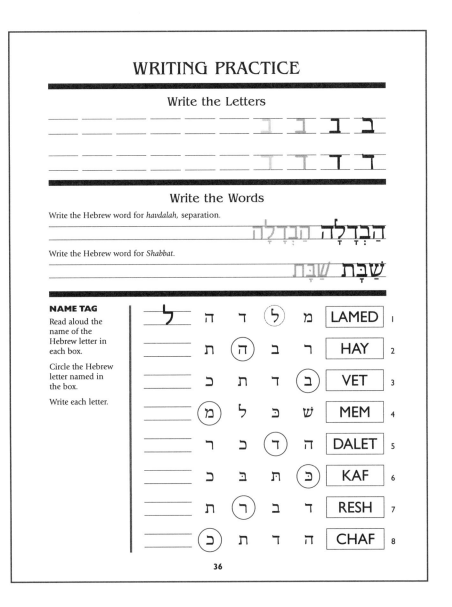

USING THE PHOTOGRAPH

What clues are there in the photograph that the family is making *havdalah*? **[wine cup, braided candle, spice box, *kippah*, *siddur*]**

THE LIVING TRADITION

Discuss together the question in the book, "What makes a week good?" At the beginning of class each week, ask the students to list what was good about the previous week.

PICTURE PERFECT

Name an object that can be used both to welcome Shabbat and to say good-bye to Shabbat? **[cup of wine]**

Make sure the students understand that it is acceptable to use grape juice instead of wine for ritual purposes. Traditionally wine has been used for Kiddush but the blessing – *borei pri hagafen* – refers not to wine specifically but more generally to "the fruit of the vine." Therefore, using grape juice for Kiddush is acceptable.

THE LIVING TRADITION הַבְדָלָה

On Saturday night, after the first three stars can be seen in the sky, שַׁבָּת comes to an end. We have a special ceremony, called הַבְדָלָה, to separate שַׁבָּת from the new week. הַבְדָלָה means "separation." In the הַבְדָלָה ceremony we use a cup of wine, a braided candle, and a box filled with sweet spices. We hope that the coming week will be a good one.

THINK ABOUT IT

What makes a week good?

PICTURE PERFECT

Write the word שַׁבָּת below the two objects we can use to welcome שַׁבָּת.

Write the word הַבְדָלָה below the two objects we can use to say good-bye to שַׁבָּת.

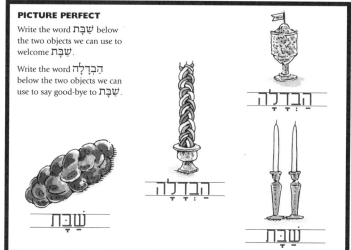

37

LESSON 6

Pages: 38–43
Key Word: וְאָהַבְתָּ
New Letters: א ו
Alef-Bet Flashcards: 17, 18
Word Cards: 10, 11

REVIEW EXERCISE

Go Fish

Put *alef-bet* flashcards #1–17 into a bag and have each child take a turn fishing out a letter and giving its name and/or sound. One of the students will choose card #17 (א). After the students come to the conclusion that they don't recognize this letter, you can explain that this is the letter to be learned in this lesson. Have that student go to the *alef-bet* chart and point out the matching letter, and then put card #17 aside until all the other cards have been fished out of the bag.

KEY WORD (וְאָהַבְתָּ)

• Which prayer tells us to love God? **[first paragraph after the Shema – *Ve'ahavta*...]**
• Why does our tradition teach us to love God? **[God created the world; God cares for us, etc.]**

If your class is familiar with the tune sung to the Ve'ahavta paragraph, sing it at this time.

INTRODUCE THE NEW LETTER – א

Once again display *alef-bet* flashcard #17 and introduce the *alef* to the class. Be sure the students understand the idea of a letter that is not sounded. If the students have difficulty with this concept, you can teach the *alef* as a letter that takes the sound of the vowel connected to it. Have the students look at the Key word in the textbook and point to the *alef*.

READING PRACTICE

Call on a student to read line 1 for the class and have the class repeat the line in unison. Repeat this procedure with lines 2 and 3.

NOW READ & READ AGAIN

Have students work in pairs reading each of the lines to each other. Listen as they practice, and correct any errors you hear.

FYI

The fourth word in line 7 of the reading practice (בְּרָאתָ) is not a mistake. There are occasional instances when an *alef* or *ayin* will not have a vowel connected to it. Generally, this occurs when a verb root ends with the letter *alef* or *ayin*.

HERITAGE WORD

Ask the students to make a list of things or people that they love. What thing is common to most of the students' lists? How is this love (אַהֲבָה) expressed?

Is God on the list? If not, you can direct the discussion to make the point that everything derives from God. For example:

– *"I love ice cream."*
– *"Where does ice cream come from?"*
– *"From milk."*
– *"Where does milk come from?"*
– *"From cows."*
– *"Where do cows come from?"*
– *"From other cows."*
– *"Where did the first cow come from?"*
– *"God."*

Students should not be made to feel defensive if God was not on their list. Indeed, you can tell them that "even if we don't put God on our list, God never stops loving us!"

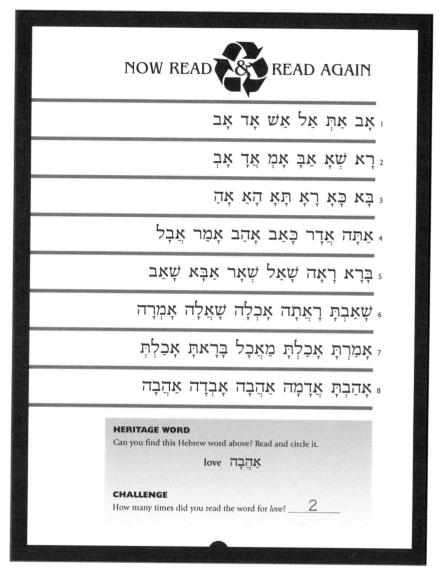

NOW READ & READ AGAIN

1 אָב אַתְ אַל אַשׁ אָד אָב

2 רָא שָׁא אַבָ אָמָ אֶדָ אָב

3 בָּא כָּא רָא תָּא הָא אָהּ

4 אַתָּה אֶדָר כָּאַב אָהַב אָמַר אֶבָל

5 בְּרָא רָאָה שָׁאַל שָׁאָר אַבָּא שָׁאַב

6 שָׁאַבְתְּ רָאָתָה אָכְלָה שָׁאֲלָה אָמְרָה

7 אָמַרְתָּ אָכַלְתָּ מַאֲכָל בְּרָאתָ אָכָלְתְּ

8 אָהַבְתָּ אֲדָמָה אַהֲבָה אָבְדָה אַהֲבָה

HERITAGE WORD
Can you find this Hebrew word above? Read and circle it.

love אַהֲבָה

CHALLENGE
How many times did you read the word for *love*? ___2___

NAME TAG

Read aloud the name of the Hebrew letter in each box and ask the students to circle the matching Hebrew letter on that line.

INTRODUCE THE NEW LETTER – ו

Using the flannelboard or chalkboard, display the letters *resh, dalet,* and *vet.* Make each letter a different color, if possible. Have the students identify their names and the sound they make. Add the *vav* and teach its name and sound. What other letter has the same sound as the *vav?* **[vet]** How does the *vav* differ in appearance from the *resh* and *dalet?*

READING PRACTICE

Ask the students to look at the Key word in the textbook, read it, define it, and name each of the letters that comprise the word.

Call on a student to read line 1 for the class and have the class repeat the line in unison. Repeat this procedure with lines 2 and 3.

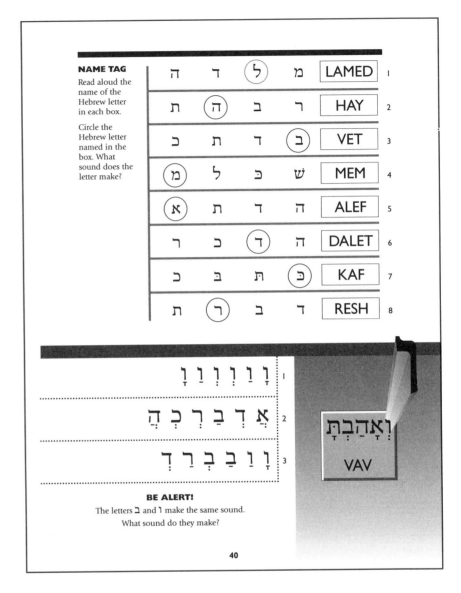

NAME TAG

Read aloud the name of the Hebrew letter in each box.

Circle the Hebrew letter named in the box. What sound does the letter make?

ה	ד	ⓛ	מ	**LAMED**	1
ת	ⓗ	ב	ר	**HAY**	2
כ	ת	ד	ⓑ	**VET**	3
ⓜ	ל	כּ	שׁ	**MEM**	4
ⓐ	ת	ד	ה	**ALEF**	5
ר	כ	ⓓ	ה	**DALET**	6
כ	ב	תּ	ⓚ	**KAF**	7
ת	ⓡ	ב	ד	**RESH**	8

1. וָ וֹ וִ וֹ וִ וָ
2. אָ דַ בַ רְ כָ הָ
3. וָ וּ בְ רַ דְ

BE ALERT!
The letters ב and ו make the same sound.
What sound do they make?

וְאָהַבְתָּ

VAV

40

NOW READ & READ AGAIN

Call out a specific word, such as "line 3, fourth word" and have a student read that word. Have the student call out the next word, or continue to call out yourself.

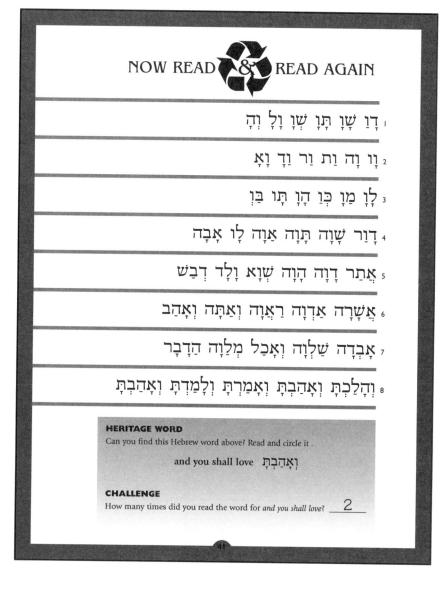

NOW READ & READ AGAIN

1. דָו שָׁו תָּו שְׁו וְל וְהָ

2. וָו וְהָ וַת וַר וַדְ וָאָ

3. לָו מַן כְּו הַו תָּו בַּו

4. דָור שָׁוָה תָּוָה אוָה לָו אָבָה

5. אַתָּר דָוָה הָוָה שָׁוָא וְלָד דְּבַשׁ

6. אַשְׁרָה אַדְוָה רַאֲוָה וְאַתָּה וְאַהַב

7. אָבְדָה שַׁלְוָה וְאָכַל מְלָוָה הַדָּבָר

8. וְהָלַכְתָּ וְאָהַבְתָּ וְאָמַרְתָּ וְלָמַדְתָּ וְאָהַבְתָּ

HERITAGE WORD
Can you find this Hebrew word above? Read and circle it .

and you shall love   וְאָהַבְתָּ

CHALLENGE
How many times did you read the word for *and you shall love*? ___2___

41

WRITE THE LETTERS

Have the students complete the writing practice exercises as in previous lessons. If teaching print writing, ensure that the students are not forming the *vav* too similarly to a *resh*.

USING THE PHOTOGRAPH

• What book do you think the boy is reading? [**siddur – prayerbook**]
• Why do you think so? [**Hebrew in book, wearing a *kippah*, etc.**]

THINK ABOUT IT

Read the translation of the Ve'ahavta paragraph (found below). You can also distribute *siddurim* to the students and show them where the Ve'ahavta is located in the prayerbook and have a student read the translation.

Ask a student to read the "Think About It" question aloud and discuss it together.

If the students have difficulty in coming up with answers to this question, have them think about the different *mitzvot* that God commands us to perform. Do they think that by performing these various *mitzvot* they are showing their love for God? Why or why not?

Love Adonai your God with all your heart, with all your soul, with all your might. And these words which I command you this day you shall take to heart. You shall diligently teach them to your children. You shall recite them at home and away, morning and night. You shall bind them as a sign upon your hand, they shall be a reminder above your eyes, and you shall inscribe them upon the doorposts of your homes and upon your gates.

THE LIVING TRADITION וְאָהַבְתָּ

וְאָהַבְתָּ means "and you shall love." The Torah teaches "to love God with all your heart, and with all your soul, and with all your might." We call this teaching the וְאָהַבְתָּ and recite it during services in the synagogue. We also write the וְאָהַבְתָּ on a piece of parchment that is put inside the *mezuzah* and hung on the doorposts of our homes.

THINK ABOUT IT

How can you show your love for God with all your heart, and with all your soul, and with all your might?

MIX AND MATCH

Draw a line to match each Hebrew term with its English meaning.

Read each Hebrew-English match aloud.

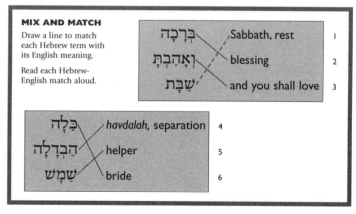

בְּרָכָה	Sabbath, rest	1
וְאָהַבְתָּ	blessing	2
שַׁבָּת	and you shall love	3
כַּלָה	*havdalah,* separation	4
הַבְדָלָה	helper	5
שַׁמָשׁ	bride	6

43

LESSON 7

Pages: 44–51
Key Word: צְדָקָה
New Letters: ק צ
Alef-Bet Flashcards: 19, 20
Word Cards: 12, 13, 14

REVIEW EXERCISE

Distribute *alef-bet* flashcards #1–18 randomly to students. Class size will determine how many cards each student receives.

Call out the name or sound of a letter or vowel and have the student with that card hold it up as it is called. Consider calling out letter/vowel combinations to add complexity to this exercise. For example, when calling the word *mar* the students with the *mem, resh, patah, kamatz,* and *hataf patah* cards should all display them.

KEY WORD (צְדָקָה)

Ask the students if they have ever heard of the Hebrew word *tsedakah*. What does it mean? **[justice]** Why is *tsedakah* important and what would the world be like if people did not perform acts of *tsedakah*?

Have the students think of causes that they would like to support (e.g., homelessness, muscular dystrophy, the environment) and have each one say and complete this sentence:

"If I had $1000, I would give it to _____ as *tsedakah*."

INTRODUCE THE NEW LETTER – ק

Point to the *kuf* on the *alef-bet* chart and ask the student holding this letter to display it. Teach the letter *kuf* and its sound. What letter already learned has the same sound? **[kaf]** Display word card #12 and point out the location of the *kuf*.

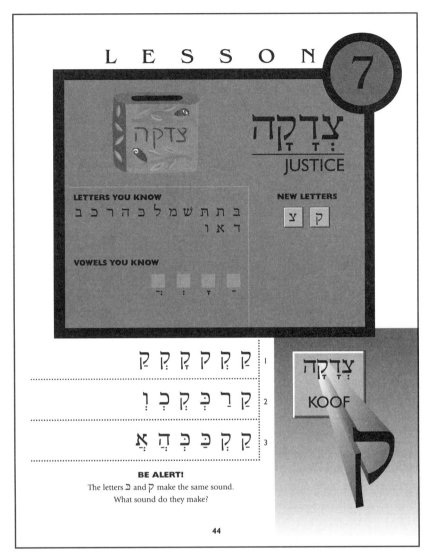

READING PRACTICE

Have the students open their books. Read the first line aloud to the class and have the students repeat the sounds in unison. Call on a student to read line 2 and then have the other students repeat in unison. Follow the same procedure for line 3.

NOW READ & READ AGAIN

Have one student read aloud all the Hebrew sounds on a line, omitting one. Another student reads the Hebrew sound that was skipped. This method encourages the students to pay attention to their classmates' reading.

HERITAGE WORDS

When are the prayers of קַבָּלַת שַׁבָּת recited? **[Friday evening]**

Kabbalat Shabbat literally means "receiving Shabbat." Why do we refer to the beginning of Shabbat as "receiving Shabbat?" Ask the students to think back to the discussion in Lesson 3 about the Shabbat *kallah.* **[Shabbat is compared to a bride and during *Kabbalat Shabbat* we welcome, or receive, the bride.]**

What song is sung during *Kabbalat Shabbat* to officially welcome the Shabbat *kallah?* **[*L'cha Dodi*]**

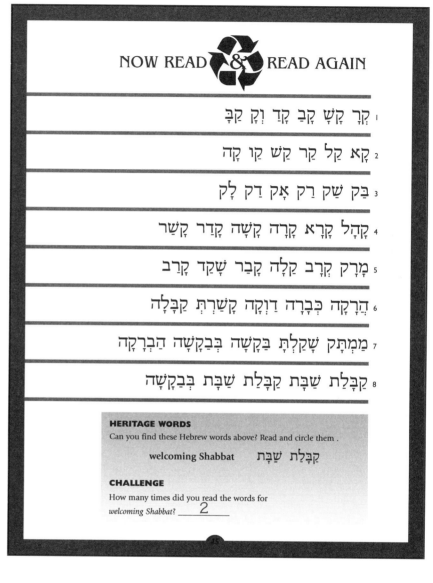

NOW READ & READ AGAIN

1 קַר קָשׁ קָב קָד וְקָ קֻבּ

2 קָא קַל קַר קַשׁ קוּ קָה

3 בַּק שַׁק רַק אָק דַק לָק

4 קָהָל קָרָא קָרָה קָשָׁה קָדַר קָשַׁר

5 מָרָק קֶרֶב קַלָּה קֶבֶר שָׁקַד קָרָב

6 הֲרָקָה כִּבְרָה דַּוְקָה קָשַׁרְתְּ קַבָּלָה

7 מַמְתָּק שָׁקַלְתָּ בַּקָשָׁה בְּבַקָשָׁה הַבְרָקָה

8 קַבָּלַת שַׁבָּת קַבָּלַת שַׁבָּת בְּבַקָשָׁה

HERITAGE WORDS

Can you find these Hebrew words above? Read and circle them .

welcoming Shabbat   קַבָּלַת שַׁבָּת

CHALLENGE

How many times did you read the words for *welcoming Shabbat?* ___2___

45

SOUND OFF

Have the students complete this exercise independently, and then review the answers together.

INTRODUCE THE NEW LETTER – צ

Display word card #12 (צְדָקָה) or look at the Key word in the book. Which letter in this word has not yet been learned? **[first letter]** Read the word slowly and ask what sound the first letter makes. **[ts]** Teach the name and review its sound. What English words have a similar sound in them? **[e.g. piz̲z̲a, boa̲t̲s, etc.]**

READING PRACTICE

Read the first line and have the students respond in unison. Call on students to first read lines 2 or 3 and then repeat it singing the sounds to a simple tune such as "Twinkle Twinkle Little Star" or "Mary Had a Little Lamb."

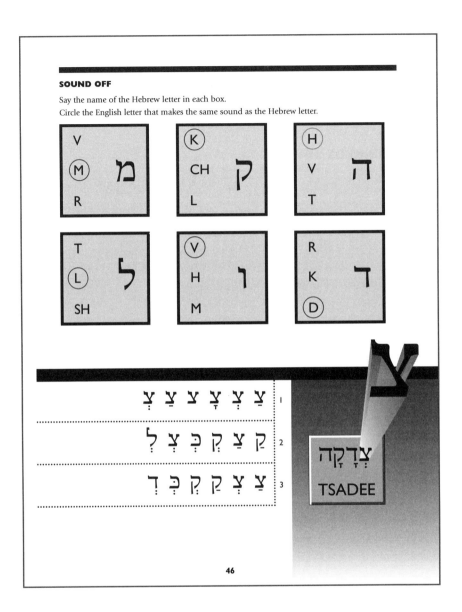

NOW READ & READ AGAIN

Have one student read a line. Then that student calls out the next line number to be read.

HERITAGE WORDS

After completing the Heritage Words exercise with the words צְדָקָה and מַצָה, teach the class about the Jewish concept of *maot ḥittim* – מָאוֹת חִטִּים. **[special funds traditionally raised by the Jewish community before *Pesaḥ* for the purpose of providing *matzot* and other Passover needs for the poor]**

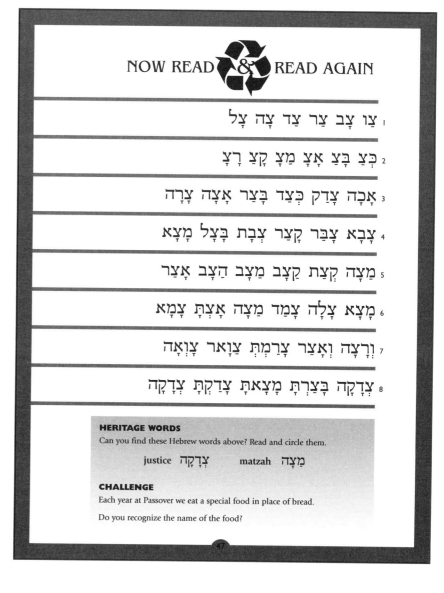

NOW READ & READ AGAIN

1 צַו צָב צַר צַד צָה צָל

2 כְּצַ בָּצַ אָצָ מַצָ קָצַ רָצָ

3 אָכָה צָדַק כִּצַד בָּצַר אָצָה צָרָה

4 צָבָא צָבַּר קָצַר צְבָת בְּצָל מָצָא

5 מַצָה קְצָת קָצָב מַצָּב הַצָּב אָצַר

6 מָצָא צָלָה צָמַד מַצָה אָצְתָ צָמָא

7 וְרָצָה וְאָצַר צָרַמְתָ צַוָּאר צַוְיאָה

8 צְדָקָה בְּצָרְתָ מְצָאתָ צָדַקְתָ צְדָקָה

HERITAGE WORDS

Can you find these Hebrew words above? Read and circle them.

justice צְדָקָה   matzah מַצָה

CHALLENGE

Each year at Passover we eat a special food in place of bread.

Do you recognize the name of the food?

47

WORD FIND

Call on students to read and define each word listed. Then have the students complete the Word Find exercise independently. For reviewing the answers, copy the puzzle onto the chalkboard (before class) and have students come to the board and circle a word from the list.

Explain to the students that the word בְּרָכָה contains the prefix הַ, which means "the."

POWER READING

Instead of having the students read the same line twice in succession, consider waiting until later in the class session or returning to this exercise in a week or two. Students should be competing against themselves and not against their classmates.

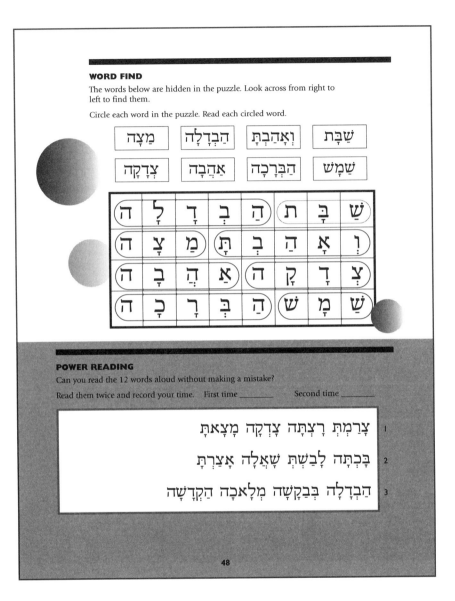

WORD FIND

The words below are hidden in the puzzle. Look across from right to left to find them.

Circle each word in the puzzle. Read each circled word.

מַצָּה	הַבְדָּלָה	וְאָהַבְתָּ	שַׁבָּת
צְדָקָה	אַהֲבָה	הַבְּרָכָה	שַׁמָּשׁ

ה	לְ	דָּ	בְּ	הַ	תָּ	בָּ	שַׁ
ה	צָ	מַ	בְ	הַ	אָ	וְ
ה	בָ	הֲ	אַ	ה	קָ	דְ	צְ
ה	כָ	רְ	בְּ	הַ	שׁ	מָ	שַׁ

POWER READING

Can you read the 12 words aloud without making a mistake?

Read them twice and record your time.   First time _____   Second time _____

1	צָרַמְתְּ רָצִתָה צְדָקָה מָצָאתָ
2	בָּכְתָה לָבַשְׁתְּ שָׁאֲלָה אָצַרְתָּ
3	הַבְדָּלָה בְּבַקָּשָׁה מְלָאכָה הַקְּדָשָׁה

48

WRITE THE LETTERS

On the chalkboard, demonstrate the technique for writing the letter *kuf*. Repeat it several times. Have the students write the letter *kuf* in the lines provided in the textbook. Ensure that the students realize that the formation of the *kuf* concludes <u>below</u> the ruled line. Repeat this procedure with the *tsadee*.

WHAT'S MISSING

After the students have completed this exercise, call on them to read and define each of the words.

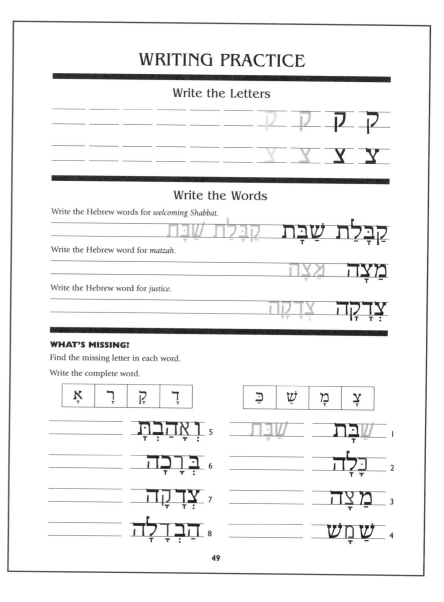

USING THE PHOTOGRAPH

What is the girl in the photograph doing? [**putting coins in a** *tsedakah* **box**]

Have the students try to read the Hebrew word on the box. [צְדָקָה]

THE LIVING TRADITION

The word *tsedakah* is often translated as "charity." However, this does not convey the true meaning of the word. Charity is a voluntary act or contribution by an individual. Judaism believes that *all* Jews – even those who receive *tsedakah* themselves – have the duty to perform acts of *tsedakah*. This idea can also be seen by the fact that the root letters of *tsedakah* – צדק – mean to act in a right or just manner.

List on the chalkboard the different acts of *tsedakah* that we can perform. Choose one *tsedakah* and, as a class, work to perform that act of *tsedakah* for the rest of the school year.

These ideas could include, but are certainly not limited to: sending get-well cards to a hospital, keeping the synagogue grounds free of litter, regularly bringing in items of food for a food bank, etc.

THE LIVING TRADITION צְדָקָה

צְדָקָה means "justice." When we help other people improve their lives, we make the world a more just and fair place. The Torah teaches us that it is our responsibility to perform acts of צְדָקָה, acts of justice to help others. One way to perform an act of צְדָקָה is to donate money to an organization that helps needy people.

THINK ABOUT IT
Can you think of other acts of צְדָקָה we can perform?

WORD MATCH
Connect each Hebrew word to its English meaning.

Read each Hebrew word and its English meaning aloud.

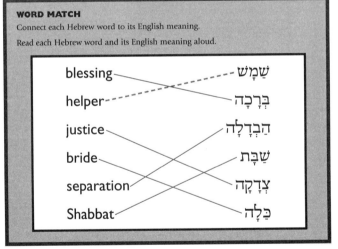

blessing — שַׁמָּשׁ

helper — בְּרָכָה

justice — הַבְדָלָה

bride — שַׁבָּת

separation — צְדָקָה

Shabbat — כַּלָּה

50

CHECKPOINT

Choose from the following techniques:

1. Have the students read the words in each box and provide the meaning if it has been learned.

2. Call out a box number at random and have the student read the word in that box.

3. Call out a Hebrew letter that has been learned and have the student read all the words in the grid that contain that letter.

4. Have the student read only words that rhyme with each other. **[1–2, 1–4, 1–5, 1–8, 1–9, 1–11, 2–4, 2–5, 2–8, 2–9, 2–11, 4–5, 4–8, 4–9, 4–11, 5–8, 5–9, 5–11, 8–9, 8–11, 9–11, 6–9, 7–10, 7–13, 10–13, 12–14]**

5. Have the student read all words that end with a *hay*. **[1, 2, 4, 5, 7, 8, 10, 11, and 13]**

FYI

Basic Checkpoint Technique

Use the Checkpoint to assess each student's progress. Listen to students read individually. Circle errors lightly in pencil in their textbooks. Reteach problem letters and retest students, erasing the pencil marks when they read the word correctly.

AN *ALEF-BET* CHART

Encourage the students to be creative in coloring in the letters on their personal *alef-bet* chart. Use different colors, designs, etc. While the students are coloring, you might play some modern Israeli music in the background to demonstrate to the students that Hebrew is a modern, living language and is not used exclusively for ritual purposes

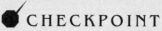

CHECKPOINT

Read the Hebrew word in each box.

אַהֲבָה 1	בְּרָכָה 2	דָּבָר 3
דְּרָשָׁה 4	הַבְדָּלָה 5	וְאָהַבְתָּ 6
כַּלָּה 7	הֲלָכָה 8	לְמַדְתָּ 9
מַצָּה 10	צְדָקָה 11	קַבָּלַת 12
רַבָּה 13	שַׁבָּת 14	תָּו 15

AN *ALEF BET* CHART
You have learned eight new letters in Lessons 4-7:
ר כ ב ד א ו ק צ
Turn to the *Alef Bet* Chart on page 160.
Color in the new letters.
How many letters do you now know? Can you name each letter?

51

LESSON 8

Pages: 52–55
Key Word: מִצְוָה
New Vowels: ִ יִ
Alef-Bet Flashcards: 21, 22
Word Cards: 15, 16, 17, 18, 19, 20

KEY WORD (מִצְוָה)

Ask the students to define the word mitzvah. Have the students make a list of all the *mitzvot* performed in a day (e.g., studying, being respectful to parents and teachers, helping the needy, washing up in the morning, etc.). They should save this list, since it will be used again at the conclusion of this lesson.

INTRODUCE THE NEW VOWEL –
(*ḤIRIK*: ִ יִ)

Write the Key word (מִצְוָה) on the chalkboard. What letter or vowel in this word has not yet been learned? [**the vowel under the *mem***] Pronounce the word מִצְוָה clearly and ask what sound they think this vowel makes. Then formally introduce this vowel and its sound.

Write on the chalkboard in random order all the vowels learned to this point. Point to each vowel and call on a student to pronounce its sound.

READING PRACTICE
Dramatic Reading

Tell the class there was once a famous actress who was so talented that she was able to bring tears to the eyes of an audience simply by reciting the alphabet. Instruct the students to read the line of syllables dramatically, as if they were on stage. For example, suggest that the first person read the line angrily, the second person sadly, and so on.

NOW READ & READ AGAIN

Call on a student to read the first three words on line 1. Then call on another student to read the next three words until all the words have been read.

When recycling this exercise, ask the students to follow these instructions for each line:

Line #	Instructions
1)	Read the words that contain a *dalet*
2)	Read the words that begin with a *hay*
3)	Read the words that contain a *alef*
4)	Read the words that contain a *bet*
5)	Read the words that contain a *kamatz*
6)	Read the words that contain a *kuf*
7)	Read the words that contain a *ḥirik*
8)	Read the word the appears three times

HERITAGE WORDS

קָדִישׁ is the name of a prayer proclaiming God's holiness and uniqueness. There are several versions of the Kaddish, recited at different points during services. The best known version is the Mourner's Kaddish. Your students may be surprised to learn that the Mourner's Kaddish makes no mention of death. It is recited by those in mourning because they are declaring their faith in God despite the loss of their loved one.

Why do you think the national anthem of Israel is called הַתִּקְוָה – The Hope? **[The Jewish People have long hoped and prayed for the return to their own land.]**

After the students have completed the exercise, ask what the significance of the צִיצִית is. **[They remind us to do God's commandments, the *mitzvot*.]**

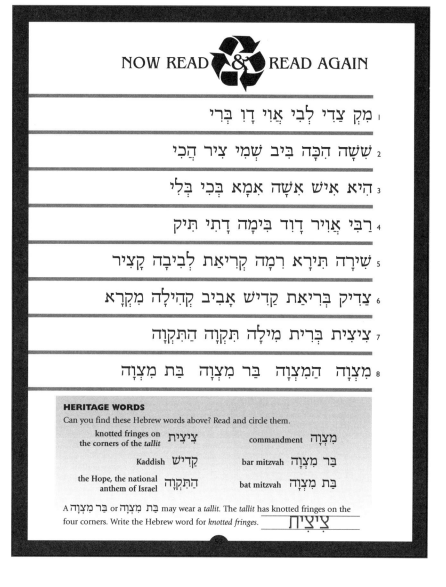

WRITING PRACTICE

This is just a reminder that *Shalom Uvrachah* [the student's edition] is available in two versions—one for teaching print writing and one for teaching script. This universal Teacher's Edition can be used with either version. You can see samples of every letter in script format on page xiv.

Choose six students to come to the chalkboard with their books and have each write one of the words twice. The rest of the class should complete the exercise in the book.

RHYME TIME

Have the students complete this exercise independently. Call on students to read aloud each of the rhyming sets.

Bingo

Have each student make a game board with nine squares. The students choose nine of the twelve words from the Rhyme Time exercise and write one in each square. The teacher calls out each of the words randomly, one by one, and the students mark off the ones on their card. The first player to cover three words across, down, or diagonal wins. This game provides both writing practice and aural word discrimination.

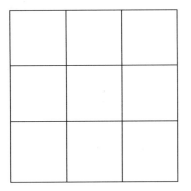

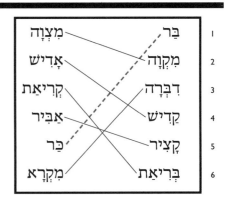

WRITING PRACTICE

Write the Words

Write the Hebrew word for *commandment.*

מִצְוָה מִצְוָה

Write the Hebrew words for *bar mitzvah.*

בַּר מִצְוָה בַּר מִצְוָה

Write the Hebrew words for *bat mitzvah.*

בַּת מִצְוָה בַּת מִצְוָה

Write the Hebrew word for *fringes on the corners of the tallit.*

צִיצִית צִיצִית

Write the Hebrew word for *Kaddish.*

קַדִּישׁ קַדִּישׁ

Write the Hebrew word for *the Hope, the national anthem of Israel.*

הַתִּקְוָה הַתִּקְוָה

RHYME TIME

Read the Hebrew words in each column.

Connect the rhyming words. Read the rhyming sets aloud.

מִצְוָה	בַּר	1
אָדִישׁ	מִקְוֶה	2
קְרִיאַת	דִּבְרָה	3
אַבִּיר	קַדִּישׁ	4
כַּר	קָצִיר	5
מִקְרָא	בְּרִיאַת	6

54

USING THE PHOTOGRAPH

What is the boy in the photograph doing? **[packing food for a food drive to help the hungry, or to take to a food bank]**

THE LIVING TRADITION

Explain that there are two types of *mitzvot*:

מִצְוֹת בֵּין אָדָם לְחֲבֵרוֹ – between humans

מִצְוֹת בֵּין אָדָם לַמָּקוֹם – between humans and God

What are examples of *mitzvot bein adam l'havero*? **[visiting the sick, giving *tsedakah*, etc.]**

What are examples of *mitzvot bein adam lamakom*? **[lighting Shabbat candles, keeping kosher, etc.]**

Have the students take the list of *mitzvot* they made at the beginning of this lesson and identify the nature of each mitzvah listed.

DISCOVER A HIDDEN WORD

Have students who complete the exercise early create their own version of this exercise by referring back to previous pages and using one of the Key or Heritage words as the "hidden word."

THE LIVING TRADITION מִצְוָה

A מִצְוָה is a commandment from God. God's commandments are written in the Torah. They tell us what we should do to follow God's laws. We do a מִצְוָה when we light Shabbat candles, hear the shofar on Rosh Hashanah, honor our parents, feed our pets, or visit a sick friend. Can you think of another מִצְוָה you can do?

DISCOVER A HIDDEN WORD

Read each line aloud.
Find and circle the Hebrew letter that is found in every word on the line.
Say the name of the letter and write it in the blank space.

בּ	דִּבְּרָה	מִדְבָּר	רַבִּי	מַלְבִּישׁ	1
ר	מִדְרַשׁ	בְּרִית	בְּקִרְבִּי	אֵרָא	2
מ	אָמַרְתִּי	בִּימָה	מִדָּה	תַּמִּיד	3
צ	מִצְוָה	צִיצִת	צָרָה	מַצִּיל	4
ן	בִּשַׁלְוָה	צוֹן	אָבִן	הִתְקַוֹן	5
ה	קְהִלָּה	אָהַבְתִּי	אִשָּׁה	לְהָבִיא	6

Write the six letters from these lines in the blank spaces:

ה ן צ מ ר בּ
6 5 4 3 2 1

Do you know what this means?

55

LESSON 9

Pages: 56–60
Key Word: שְׁמַע
New Letter: ע
Alef-Bet Flashcard: 23
Word Cards: 21, 22

REVIEW EXERCISE

Packing Grandmother's Suitcase

Play the "Grandmother's Suitcase" game described in #6 on page viii. Use flashcards #1–22. If you are not teaching the names of the vowels, have the students say the vowel sounds.

KEY WORD (שְׁמַע)

Hold up word card #21 (שְׁמַע) and say, "I packed my grandmother's suitcase and in it I put the Shema." Do the students recognize this word? From where? What does it mean? **[hear]**

Sing the Shema together. How do you feel when you sing the *Shema*?

Why is the Shema one of the most important prayers in Judaism? **[It declares our belief and faith in our God, the only God. Some people refer to the Shema as the Jewish pledge of allegiance.]**

INTRODUCE THE NEW LETTER – ע

Point out the *ayin* on word card #21 and explain that this is another letter that is not sounded. Ask a student to come up to the *alef-bet* chart and point to another letter that is not sounded. **[*alef*]**

READING PRACTICE

Have the students read the sounds on the three lines vertically. There will be six columns of three words each. Call on students at random to read the columns.

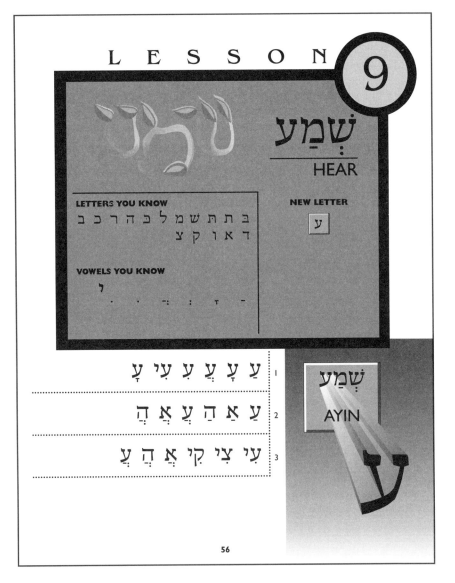

FYI

In the Sephardic tradition the *ayin* is pronounced as a guttural.

NOW READ & READ AGAIN

Call on students at random to read each of the lines. Encourage students to concentrate on their classmates' reading by having them follow the reading with their fingers. Suddenly stop the reading to see who has their finger at the correct spot. Praise those who have the place. Don't forget to recycle.

HERITAGE WORDS

The Hebrew word for "Hebrew" is עִבְרִית. Why is it important to learn how to read Hebrew? **[to be able to read the prayerbook, Torah, etc.]**

What two words in line 8 seem to be related to the word שְׁמַע ? **[you will hear – תִּשְׁמַע , hearing – שְׁמִיעָה]**

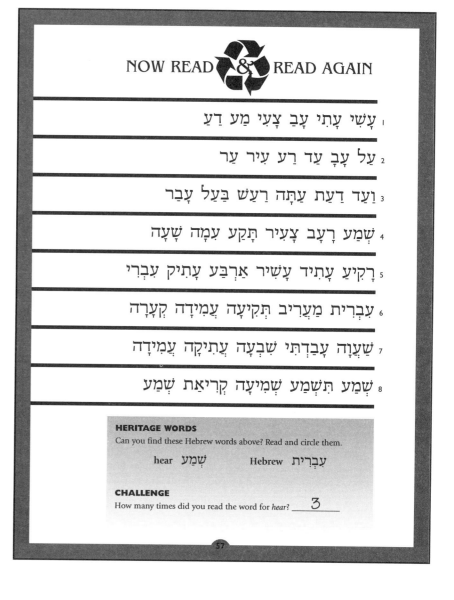

NOW READ & READ AGAIN

1. עָשִׂי עָתִי עָב צָעִי מַע דַע
2. עַל עָבְ עַד רַע עִיר עַר
3. וַעַד דַעַת עַתָּה רַעַשׁ בַּעַל עָבַר
4. שְׁמַע רָעָב צָעִיר תָּקַע עִמָּה שָׁעָה
5. רָקִיעַ עָתִיד עָשִׁיר אַרְבַּע עָתִיק עִבְרִי
6. עִבְרִית מַעֲרִיב תְּקִיעָה עֲמִידָה קְעָרָה
7. שַׁעֲוָה עֲבַדְתִּי שִׁבְעָה עֲתִיקָה עֲמִידָה
8. שְׁמַע תִּשְׁמַע שְׁמִיעָה קְרִיאַת שְׁמַע

HERITAGE WORDS
Can you find these Hebrew words above? Read and circle them.

hear שְׁמַע   Hebrew עִבְרִית

CHALLENGE
How many times did you read the word for *hear*? ___3___

57

POWER READING

Complete this exercise as directed in the book. Remember to emphasize that the students are competing against themselves and not against their classmates.

This might be a good time to go back to the Power Reading exercise in Lesson 7 (page 48) and retime the students on reading those lines.

SOUNDS LIKE

Have the students complete the exercise independently. When everyone has finished, call on students to read each line aloud and provide their answer.

POWER READING

Can you read all the words aloud without making a mistake?

Read them twice and record your time.

First time _____   Second time _____

בַּעַל	שָׁעָה	לָמַד	צָעַד	1
שָׁעַל	שַׁעַר	עָמַד	בָּקַע	2
הִשְׁמִיעַ	עֲרִירִי	בִּשְׁעַת	בְּרֶעָשׁ	3
עָמְדָה	עֲבַדְתָּ	וְעָצַר	עֲמִידָה	4
אַרְבָּעָה	לְהַקְדִּישׁ	וְאָהַבְתָּ	וְדִבַּרְתָּ	5
וְאָכַלְתָּ	וְאָמַרְתָּ	וְהָאֲדָמָה	וַעֲבַדְתָּ	6

SOUNDS LIKE

Read the Hebrew word in each box.

Read the Hebrew sounds on each line.

Circle the Hebrew sound on each line that sounds the same as the Hebrew in the box.

צֶב	רַב	עֶב	צֶו	1
צָבָא	קָרַע	רְקַע	קְרָא	2
אַתָּה	צָמָא	עָמָה	אִמָּא	3
אָשִׁיר	עָתִיד	אֲוִיר	עָשִׁיר	4
צָמָה	מָצָא	צַעַד	מַצָּה	5
הָדָד	דָּוִר	הָדַר	דָּבָר	6

58

WRITE THE LETTER

On the chalkboard, demonstrate the technique for writing the letter *ayin*. Repeat it several times. Have the students write the letter *ayin* in the lines provided in the textbook. If you are teaching print writing, ensure that the students realize that part of the formation of the *ayin* is <u>slightly below</u> the ruled line.

WORD FIND

Read the instructions and have the students complete the exercise independently

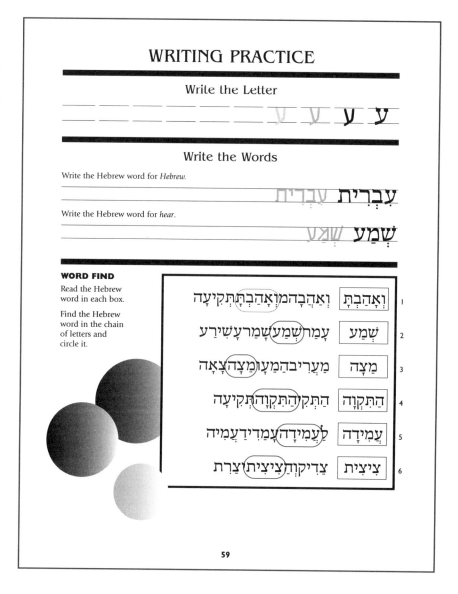

WRITING PRACTICE

Write the Letter

ע   ע   ע

Write the Words

Write the Hebrew word for *Hebrew*.

עִבְרִית   עברית

Write the Hebrew word for *hear*.

שְׁמַע   שׁמע

WORD FIND

Read the Hebrew word in each box.

Find the Hebrew word in the chain of letters and circle it.

וְאָהַבְתָּ   וְאָהֲבָהַמוֹּאָהַבְתָּתְּקִיעָה   1

שְׁמַע   עָמַרְשְׁמַעְשְׁמַּרעָשִׁירַע   2

מַצָה   מַעֲרִיבהַמַעְוֹמַצָהצָאָה   3

הַתִּקְוָה   הַתִּקְהַתִּקְוָהתְּקִיעָה   4

עֲמִידָה   לַעֲמִידָהעֲמַדִידַעֲמִיה   5

צִיצִית   צַדִיקוֹהַצִיצִיתצָרת   6

59

USING THE PHOTOGRAPH

- What prayer do you think these children are reciting? **[Shema]**
- How do you know? **[they have their eyes closed]**

THE LIVING TRADITION

The most common reason given for closing your eyes during the Shema is to keep out distractions so you can concentrate on the meaning of the prayer.

Have your students practice saying the Shema with eyes open and then closed. Have them note what they felt the differences were. **[e.g., feeling more private, feeling alone, feeling God's presence, sharpens our hearing, etc.]**

THE LIVING TRADITION שְׁמַע

The Hebrew word שְׁמַע means "hear." שְׁמַע is the first word in one of our most important prayers. This prayer is called the שְׁמַע. Its words are found in the Torah. When we recite the שְׁמַע we declare our belief in One God by saying: "Hear O Israel, Adonai is our God, Adonai is One."

PICTURE PERFECT

Read each word.

Write the correct word below the matching picture.

צְדָקָה
שְׁמַע
עִבְרִית
כַּלָה
צִיצִית

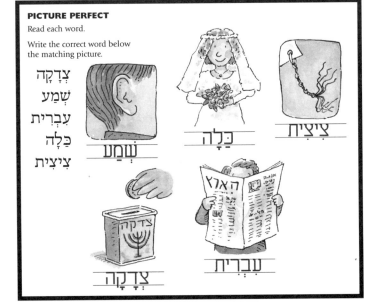

60

LESSON 10

Pages: 61–65
Key Word: נָבִיא
New Letters: נ ן
Alef-Bet Flashcards: 24, 25
Word Card: 23

KEY WORD (נָבִיא)

What is a prophet? [**In English the word "prophet" may mean someone with magical powers who can foretell the future. In Hebrew, the word *navi* means someone who speaks out as a messenger of God.**]

Why were the prophets important? [**They told us how God wanted us to behave, even if that message did not always please the Jewish people, and they gave hope to the Jewish people when they felt sad or confused.**]

Can you name any prophets? [**e.g., Moses, Elijah, Jeremiah, Isaiah, etc.**]

INTRODUCE THE NEW LETTERS – נ ן

Show word card #23 (נָבִיא) or print the word on the chalkboard and read it. Which letter in the word have they not learned? Display *alef-bet* flashcard #24 (נ) to the class and ask if any of the students know this letter. (a few may know the letter from the Ḥanukkah dreidel) Teach the name of the letter and its sound.

Next, display *alef-bet* flashcard #25 (ן). Teach the name of this letter and its sound. Explain to students that *final nun* will be found only at the end of a word.

Occasionally some letters can be confusing to the students because of their similar appearance. Add flashcards #11, 12, 15, and 18 (ר כ ד ו) to the two new cards for this lesson and drill the students on these six look-alike letters.

LESSON TEN

READING PRACTICE

Read line 1 for the class and have them repeat the line in unison. Call on a student to read line 2 and then have the entire class repeat in unison. Repeat this procedure with line 3.

NOW READ & READ AGAIN

Have a student read until you clap your hands. At that time, have the next student read. Determine the number of words according to the student's ability and reading fluency, keeping the pace lively.

HERITAGE WORDS

Which *navi* played a major role in the story of *Pesah?* **[Moses]**

Which *navi* do we welcome into our homes during the Passover seder. Hint: We have a special cup for him to drink from. **[Elijah]**

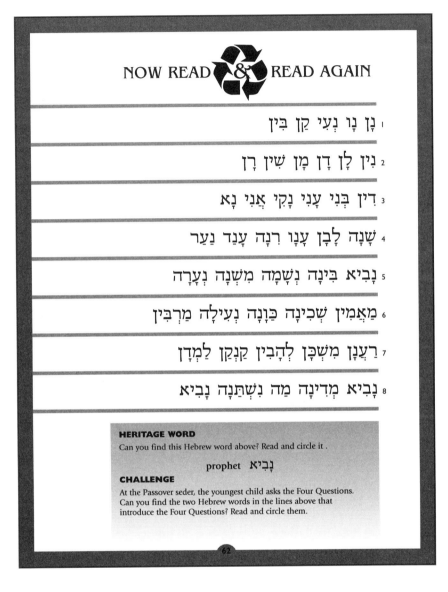

NOW READ & READ AGAIN

1 נָן נָו נְעִי קַן בִּין

2 נִין לָן דָן מָן שִׁין רָן

3 דִין בְּנִי עָנִי נָקִי אֲנִי נָא

4 שָׁנָה לָבָן עָנָו רִנָה עָנַד נַעַר

5 נָבִיא בִּינָה נְשָׁמָה מִשְׁנָה נְעָרָה

6 מַאֲמִין שְׁכִינָה כַּוָנָה נְעִילָה מַרְבִּין

7 רַעֲנָן מִשְׁכָּן לְהָבִין קַנְקַן לַמְדָן

8 נָבִיא מְדִינָה מַה נִשְׁתַּנָה נָבִיא

HERITAGE WORD

Can you find this Hebrew word above? Read and circle it.

prophet נָבִיא

CHALLENGE

At the Passover seder, the youngest child asks the Four Questions. Can you find the two Hebrew words in the lines above that introduce the Four Questions? Read and circle them.

62

SEARCH AND CIRCLE

Have the students complete this exercise independently. Call on students at random to provide their answer and also have that student write the correct sounds on the chalkboard.

SOUNDS LIKE

Read all the sounds on each line and have the students circle the sounds on each line that are the same.

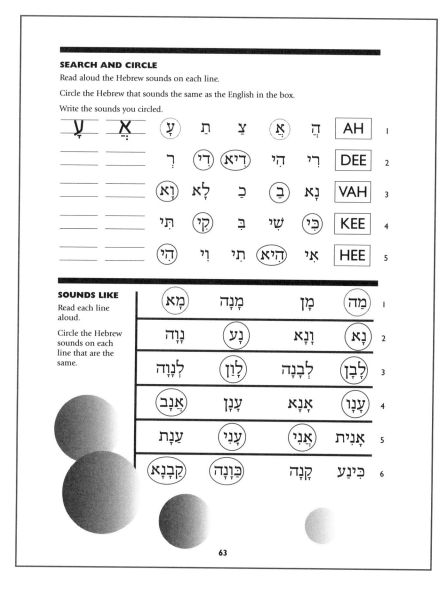

WRITE THE LETTERS

Have the students complete the writing practice exercises as in previous lessons. Ensure that the students are writing the *final nun* so that it finishes <u>below</u> the ruled line and that they are not making the *final nun* too similar to a *vav*.

NUN ADD-IN

Have the students complete the exercise independently. Walk around the room to check on their work.

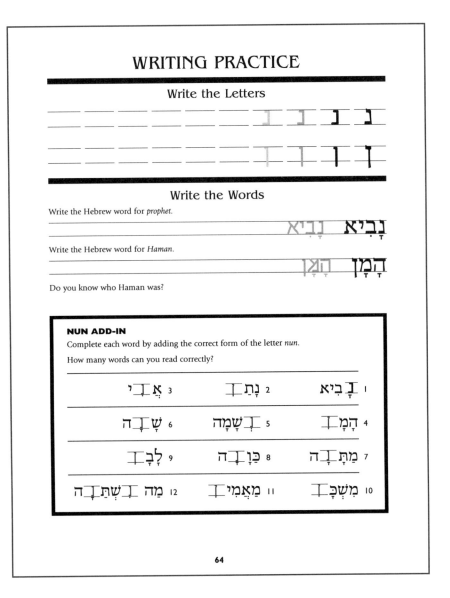

USING THE PHOTOGRAPH

- Where is Moses standing? **[in front of the burning bush]**
- Why is he not wearing any shoes? **[God told him to remove his shoes because it was a holy place]**
- What did God tell Moses to do at this time? **[return to Egypt to lead the people out of slavery]**

THE LIVING TRADITION

What do you think it would feel like to be a prophet – a messenger for God? Imagine that you are Moses and that you are approaching Pharaoh for the first time to ask for the freedom of the Israelites from slavery. How would you feel and what would you say? Have the students work in pairs or groups of three and write a skit reenacting this scene.

Before eliciting responses, give the students the following information: The *ne'viim* were sometimes reluctant to act as God's messengers but they felt compelled to deliver God's word to the Jewish people because they believed that they had been chosen by God for this duty.

WORD POWER

Ask the students if they know the meaning of any of the other Hebrew words, in addition to the ones defined as part of this exercise. The following are the definitions of all the words.

קְרִיאַת - reading of...	כַּוָּנָה - intention; spiritual intensity	עִבְרִית - Hebrew	שָׁנָה - year
נָבִיא - prophet	אַרְבַּע - four	מַעֲרִיב - evening service	שְׁכִינָה - God's presence
בְּרִית - covenant; circumcision	וְאָהַבְתָּ - and you shall love	תְּקִיעָה - sounding; Shofar call	נְשָׁמָה - Soul
מִצְוָה - commandment	אַהֲבָה - love	אִמָּא - mother	קַדִּישׁ - Kaddish
נְעִילָה - closing; final service on Yom Kippur	מִשְׁכָּן - tabernacle	הַתִּקְוָה - the Hope; Israel's national anthem	קַבָּלַת - welcoming of...

THE LIVING TRADITION נָבִיא

The Hebrew word נָבִיא means "prophet." In the days of the Bible a נָבִיא was a spokesperson for God. The נָבִיא gave hope to our people when they felt sad and lost. These are the names of some of our prophets: Joshua, Isaiah, Jeremiah, Ezekiel, Hosea, and Deborah. Our first and greatest נָבִיא was Moses.

WORD POWER

Read aloud the Hebrew words on each line. Circle the word that has the same meaning as the English word(s) in the box.

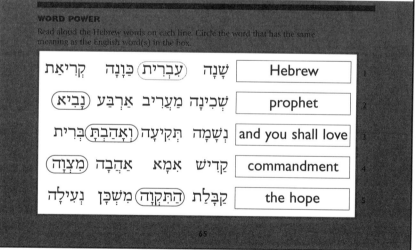

קְרִיאַת	כַּוָּנָה	(עִבְרִית)	שָׁנָה	Hebrew
שְׁכִינָה	מַעֲרִיב	אַרְבַּע	(נָבִיא)	prophet
נְשָׁמָה	תְּקִיעָה	(וְאָהַבְתָּ)	בְּרִית	and you shall love
קַדִּישׁ	אִמָּא	אַהֲבָה	(מִצְוָה)	commandment
קַבָּלַת	(הַתִּקְוָה)	מִשְׁכָּן	נְעִילָה	the hope

65

It is valuable for the students to realize that at this point in their Hebrew studies the majority of the sounds they are reading are actual Hebrew words.

LESSON 11

Pages: 66–70
Key Word: חַלָה
New Letter: ח
Alef-Bet Flashcard: 26
Word Cards: 24, 25

KEY WORD (חַלָה)

Display word cards #1 (שַׁבָּת), #6 (בְּרָכָה), and #15 (מִצְוָה), and have the students read and define each word. Then ask, "What *brachah* do we recite on *Shabbat* to fulfill the *mitzvah* of eating *ḥallah*?"

בָּרוּךְ אַתָּה ה' אֱלֹהֵינוּ מֶלֶךְ הָעוֹלָם, הַמּוֹצִיא לֶחֶם מִן הָאָרֶץ.

INTRODUCE THE NEW LETTER – ח

Print a large *hay* on the chalkboard and have the class identify the letter. Then print a large *ḥet* next to the *hay*. How do these two letters differ in appearance? Introduce the letter *ḥet*. What other letter is pronounced the same way? [כ]

Have the students look in their textbooks at the Key word. What is the first letter? [*ḥet*] Ask for a volunteer to read the word.

Take a poll. Who likes their *ḥallah* plain; with raisins; with poppy seeds; with sesame seeds? Does anyone else have a different favorite type of *ḥallah*?

FYI

Sephardic tradition distinguishes between the *ḥet* and the *chaf* by pronouncing the *ḥet* in a more guttural way.

READING PRACTICE

Randomly call on students to read each of these three lines. Remember, these lines can be repeated to give more students a chance to read.

NOW READ & READ AGAIN

Tape-record each student as he or she reads one of the lines. Two or three weeks later have the students, in the same order, read the same line on a second tape. Play back both and compare. This method allows the students to hear proof of their improvement.

HERITAGE WORDS

In what prayer do we use the word הָרַחֲמָן numerous times? [**Birkat Hamazon – Grace after Meals**]

Get a copy of *Birkat HaMazon* with translation and read to the students in Hebrew and then in English a few of the blessings that begin with the word *haraḥaman*. What other word usually begins a blessing? [**baruch**]

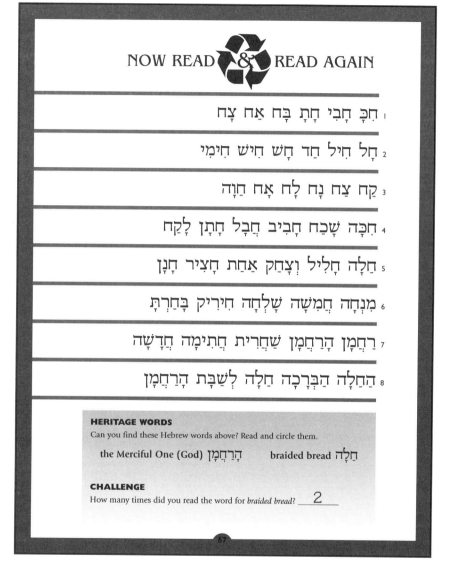

NOW READ & READ AGAIN

1 חַךְ חָבִי חָתָ בָּה אַח צָח

2 חָל חִיל חַד חָשׁ חִישׁ חִימִי

3 קַח צָח נָח לָח אָח חַוָה

4 חִכָּה שָׁכַח חָבִיב חֶבֶל חָתָן לָקַח

5 חַלָּה חָלִיל וְצָחַק אַחַת חָצִיר חָנָן

6 מִנְחָה חֲמִשָּׁה שָׁלְחָה חִירִיק בַּחֲרָתְ

7 רַחֲמָן הָרַחֲמָן שַׁחֲרִית חֲתִימָה חֲדָשָׁה

8 הַחַלָּה הַבְּרָכָה חַלָּה לְשַׁבָּת הָרַחֲמָן

HERITAGE WORDS
Can you find these Hebrew words above? Read and circle them.

the Merciful One (God) הָרַחֲמָן   braided bread חַלָּה

CHALLENGE
How many times did you read the word for *braided bread*? __2__

67

LETTER AND VOWEL KNOW-HOW

Following are five different options for practicing this page:

1. Call on students to read across the rows (1-18).

2. Have students read down the columns (1-5).

3. Call on students at random to read each of the lines and to identify the name and sound of each letter.

4. Allow students to work in small groups and to take turns reading complete lines and correcting each other.

5. Have the students roll three dice and read the line number equivalent to the sum of the numbers on the dice. (Since 3 will be the lowest number possible, read lines 1 and 2 in unison.)

WRITING THE LETTER

Have the students complete the writing practice exercises as in previous lessons. Ensure that the students are not making the *ḥet* too similarly to a *hay*.

RHYME TIME

Have the students complete this exercise independently. Call on students to read aloud each of the rhyming sets. Call on another student to read the word on each line that does not rhyme.

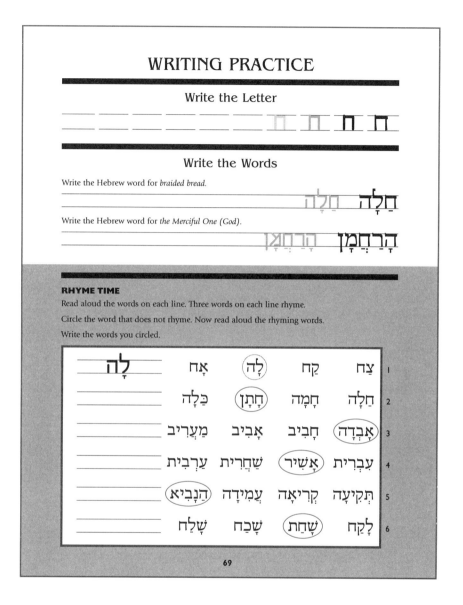

WRITING PRACTICE

Write the Letter

Write the Words

Write the Hebrew word for *braided bread*.

חַלָּה

Write the Hebrew word for *the Merciful One (God)*.

הָרַחֲמָן

RHYME TIME

Read aloud the words on each line. Three words on each line rhyme.

Circle the word that does not rhyme. Now read aloud the rhyming words.

Write the words you circled.

לָה	אָח	לָה	קַח	צַח	1
	כַּלָּה	חָתָן	חָמָה	חַלָּה	2
	מַעֲרִיב	אָבִיב	חָבִיב	אֲבֹדָה	3
	עַרְבִית	שַׁחֲרִית	אַשִׁיר	עִבְרִית	4
	הַנָּבִיא	עֲמִידָה	קְרִיאָה	תְּקִיעָה	5
	שָׁלַח	שָׁכַח	שָׁחַת	לָקַח	6

69

USING THE PHOTOGRAPH

- Why are there two *ḥallot* in the photograph? **[It reminds us that when the Israelites were wandering in the desert, God provided them with daily portions of a sweet-tasting food called *manna*. But before Shabbat, God provided a double portion so the Israelities would not have to gather food on Shabbat.]**
- How do you think this girl is feeling? Why?

THE LIVING TRADITION

Why do some people put salt on their *ḥallah* after reciting the *brachah*? **[reminder of the salt that the Priests used to put on the sacrifices in the ancient Temple]**

Make or purchase *ḥallah* dough before class and have the students make their own *ḥallah* rolls. Have sesame or poppy seeds available for sprinkling on top.

WORD SKILLS

After students complete this exercise independently, have them write their own English sentences using these Hebrew words.

THE LIVING TRADITION חַלָה

חַלָה is the special bread we eat on שַׁבָּת. The dough is usually braided or twisted before it is baked. When we welcome שַׁבָּת we recite a בְּרָכָה over חַלָה, as well as over candles and wine.

CHALLENGE
Can you recite each בְּרָכָה that we say when we welcome שַׁבָּת?

WORD SKILLS
Read the Hebrew words below. Write the correct Hebrew word above its English meaning. Read the sentence using the Hebrew word.

בְּרָכָה	חַלָה	שְׁמַע
נָבִיא	צְדָקָה	מִצְוָה

1. We say a בְּרָכָה (blessing) to say *Thank You* to God.

2. It is a מִצְוָה (commandment) to help feed the hungry.

3. We eat חַלָה (braided bread) on שַׁבָּת.

4. A נָבִיא (prophet) was a spokesperson for God.

5. We say the prayer שְׁמַע (Hear) *O Israel, Adonai is our God, Adonai is One* in the morning service and the evening service.

6. When we perform an act of צְדָקָה (justice), we are following God's commandments.

70

LESSON 12

Pages: 71–74
Key Word: עֲלִיָה
New Letter: י
Alef-Bet Flashcard: 27
Word Cards: 26, 27

KEY WORD (עֲלִיָה)

- What does it mean when someone receives an עֲלִיָה to the Torah? **[They will recite the blessings before and after the ritual reading of the Torah in the synagogue.]**
- Why do you think being called up to recite the blessings over the Torah is called *aliyah* – going up? Where is the Torah read from? **[the bimah]** How do you get to the *bimah*? **[walk up several steps]** Also, we are raised up spiritually when we are honored by reciting the blessings over the Torah.

INTRODUCE THE NEW LETTER – י

Print the Key word on the chalkboard. Are there any letters or vowels in the word which the students have not seen before? **[no]** Point to the *yud* and ask what vowel this is part of. **[*hirik* – יִ]** Explain that in addition to being part of a vowel sound, the *yud* can also stand alone as a letter. Demonstrate the sound of the *yud* and then read the Key word to the class.

Hold up *alef-bet* flashcards #11, 18, and 25 (ר ו ן) next to *alef-bet* flashcard #27 (י). Ask how each of these letters differs from the *yud*. How can you tell when the *yud* is part of a vowel and when it stands alone as a letter? **[The *yud* is read as a letter when it has a vowel directly underneath it. E.g., יְ vs. אִי]** Remember to also teach the pronunciation of the sound pattern יִ.

READING PRACTICE

Randomly call on students to read each of these three lines. Remember, these lines can be repeated to give more students a chance to read.

NOW READ & READ AGAIN

Have students read three words at a time. The first student reads three words. The second student overlaps by beginning with the previous student's last word.

HERITAGE WORDS

A מִנְיָן is needed for the Torah to be read and therefore for someone to receive an *aliyah* to the Torah.

Why are there certain rituals or prayers that can be done only with a *minyan*? **[Ten people represent a community. There are some rituals and prayers that are so important, we want to do them only when a community of people is present. Also, by praying in a group we think about other people as well as ourselves.]**

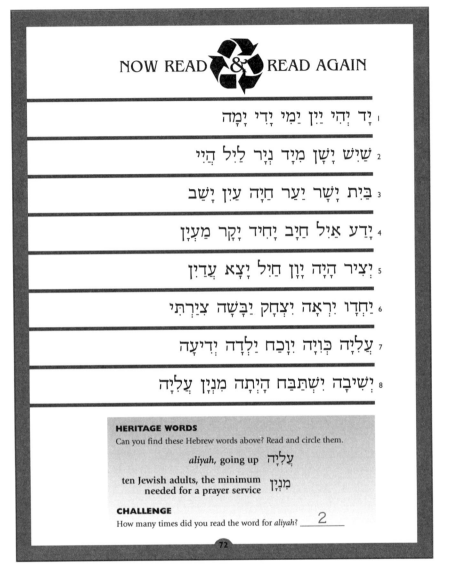

NOW READ & READ AGAIN

1 יָד יְהִי יַיִן יָמַי יְדֵי יָמָה

2 שַׁיִשׁ יָשָׁן מִיָד נִיר לַיִל הֵיִי

3 בַּיִת יָשָׁר יַעַר חַיָּה עַיִן יָשַׁב

4 יָדַע אַיִל חַיָּב יָחִיד יָקָר מַעְיָן

5 יְצִיר הָיָה יַיִן חַיִל יָצָא עֲדַיִן

6 יַחְדָּו יִרְאָה יִצְחָק יַבָּשָׁה צִיַּרְתִּי

7 עֲלִיָּה כִּוִיָּה יוֹכַח יַלְדָּה יְדִיעָה

8 יְשִׁיבָה יִשְׁתַּבַּח הָיְתָה מִנְיָן עֲלִיָּה

HERITAGE WORDS

Can you find these Hebrew words above? *Read and circle them.*

aliyah, going up   עֲלִיָּה

ten Jewish adults, the minimum needed for a prayer service   מִנְיָן

CHALLENGE

How many times did you read the word for *aliyah*? _____ 2

72

LESSON TWELVE

72

WRITING PRACTICE

This is another friendly reminder that *Shalom Uvrachah* [the student's edition] is available in two versions—one for teaching print writing and one for teaching script. This universal Teacher's Edition can be used with either version. You can see samples of every letter in script format on page xiv.

WRITING PRACTICE

Have the students complete the writing practice exercises as in previous lessons. Ensure that the students are not bringing the "tail" of the *yud* too far down.

YUD DETECTIVE

Call on students randomly to read each line aloud. Then have the students complete the "challenge" independently. You can adapt the challenge by having the students circle <u>every</u> word where the *yud* is part of a vowel. Walk around the classroom and quietly offer assistance to those students who have difficulty with this portion of the exercise.

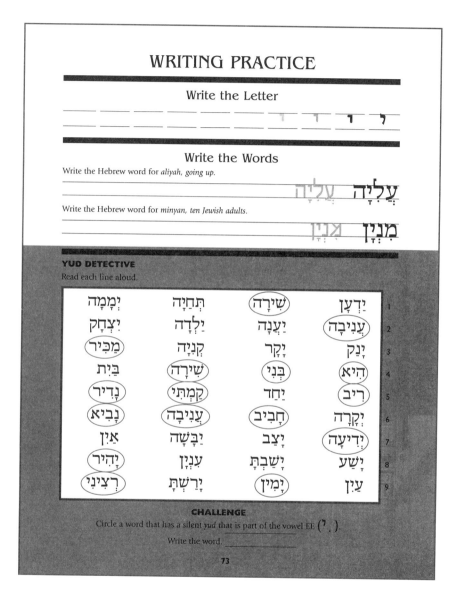

USING THE PHOTOGRAPH

- From where are these people walking? **[an airplane]**
- Where do you think they have traveled to? **[Israel]** How do you know? **[Israeli flag]**

THE LIVING TRADITION

Why do we use the word *aliyah* for someone who moves to Israel? **[Since Israel is considered the Holy Land, moving from another country to the Holy Land is considered "going up" or increasing in holiness. An analogy to this is that someone who receives a promotion in a company is considered "moving up" in the company.]**

The last part of the blessings recited before and after the Torah reading, by the person honored with an *aliyah* reads –

בָּרוּךְ אַתָּה ה׳ נוֹתֵן הַתּוֹרָה.
Blessed is Adonai who gives the Torah.

Why do you think the Jewish people is so grateful for receiving the Torah? **[teaches us our history, helps us to be moral people, allows us to be partners with God, etc.]**

CONNECTIONS

Have the students complete this exercise independently. Then call on one student to read the opening word-part and another student to read the concluding word-part.

Another option is to play a matching game. Distribute cards with the beginning of the word to some students and cards with the ending of the word to the other students. Students find a match for their part of the word. At the end of the game, everyone should be standing in pairs.

THE LIVING TRADITION עֲלִיָּה

In the synagogue, the honor of being called up to the Torah is known as an עֲלִיָּה. The word עֲלִיָּה means "going up." We go up to the *bimah* and recite blessings before and after each section of the Torah is read.

The word עֲלִיָּה has another meaning. If someone moves to Israel, we say that person has made עֲלִיָּה, because the person has gone up to the land of Israel, the Holy Land.

CONNECTIONS

Read aloud the word-parts in each column.

Draw lines to connect the beginning of a word in the right-hand column to its ending in the left-hand column.

Read each completed word aloud.

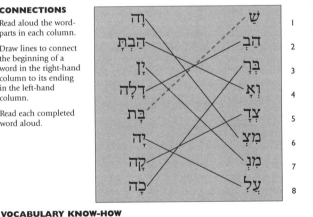

וֶה	שֶׁ	1
הַבְּתָ	הַב	2
יֵן	בְּךָ	3
דְלָה	וְאָ	4
בָּת	צְךָ	5
יָּה	מְצָ	6
קָה	מְנַ	7
כָה	עַל	8

VOCABULARY KNOW-HOW
Do you know the Hebrew word for *justice?* Write it here.   צְדָקָה

74

LESSON 13

Pages: 75–80
Key Word: לְחַיִּים
New Letter: ם
Alef-Bet Flashcard: 28
Word Cards: 28, 29, 30

REVIEW EXERCISE

Utilizing word cards #1–27 (each of the Key and Heritage words learned up to this point), post a column of at least six words. Individuals or teams take turns "climbing the ladder" by reading and translating the words on the ladder. Score one point for each word read correctly and an additional two points for each word translated correctly.

INTRODUCE THE NEW LETTER – ם

Ask the students which letter has a special form that is used only as the last letter in a word. [ן] Then point to the *mem* on the *alef-bet* chart and ask for a volunteer to identify it. Explain that the *mem* also has a special form used only at the end of a word and then point to the *final mem* on the *alef-bet* chart.

KEY WORD (לְחַיִּים)

Print the word לְחַיִּים on the chalkboard or show word card #28 and ask for a volunteer to read it. Is this word familiar to anyone? Explain that *l'ḥayyim* is not actually a word, but a phrase. Put one circle around the לְ and another one around חַיִּים. Explain that לְ is the preposition meaning "to" and חַיִּים means "life."

You may want to ask the challenge question found at the bottom of the following page at this time. "When would you say *l'ḥayyim*?"

READING PRACTICE

Call on students randomly to read each of the three lines.

LESSON THIRTEEN

NOW READ & READ AGAIN

Change the line sequence by first reading all the odd-numbered lines followed by the even-numbered lines.

HERITAGE WORDS

In some contexts the word אָדָם refers to humans in general, and not only males. This is similar to statements such as "All men are created equal," which refers to all humanity.

What was the name of the first woman? **[Eve – חַוָּה – who gave birth (life) to future generations.]**

Why do we recall יְצִיאַת מִצְרַיִם every Shabbat? Indeed, it is part of many of our Shabbat prayers, including the Kiddush. **[The verse from the Ten Commandments telling us to observe Shabbat says that we should "remember that you were a slave in the land of Egypt and that *Adonai*, your God, set you free." As slaves the Israelites had no day of rest.]**

NOW READ & READ AGAIN

1 הָלַם אַחִים עָלִים מִרְיָם בַּדִּים תָּרַם

2 אִיִּים שְׁנַיִם בָּתִּים אָדָם דַּקִּים מִצְרַיִם

3 חָכָם רַעַם יָמִים רַבִּים חַיִּים דָּמַם

4 בָּנִים מַיִם אָדָם שְׁתַּיִם מִלִּים אָשַׁם

5 נָשִׁים שָׁמַיִם דְּבָרִים יָדַיִם קָמִים עָלִים

6 אַבְרָהָם נְבִיאִים כְּרָמִים שִׁבְעִים אֲנָשִׁים

7 עִבְרִים רַחֲמִים יְלָדִים צַדִּיקִים מְלָכִים

8 עֲבָדִים יְצִיאַת מִצְרַיִם לְחַיִּים לְחַיִּים

HERITAGE WORDS

Can you find these Hebrew words above? Read and circle them.

to life לְחַיִּים

the name of the first human (man) אָדָם

the Exodus, going out from Egypt יְצִיאַת מִצְרַיִם

CHALLENGE

Jewish people say לְחַיִּים on very special occasions.

When would you say לְחַיִּים?

Call on students to read each of the words. Before class, copy the puzzle onto the chalkboard and call on students individually to come to the board and circle one of the words on the list.

WORD FIND

Read each word aloud. The words are hidden in the puzzle. Look across from right to left to find them. Circle each word you find.

מִנְחָה	צִיצִת	שְׁמַע	מִצְוָה
צְדָקָה	הָרַחֲמָן	הַתִּקְוָה	קַדִּישׁ
מִנְיָן	נְשָׁמָה	כַּוָּנָה	בְּרִית
	שַׁבָּת	כַּלָּה	

כ	ו	נ	ה	צ	ד	ק	ה
ב	ר	י	ת	מ	צ	ו	ה
שׁ	מ	ע	ה	ת	ק	ו	ה
ק	ד	י	שׁ	מ	נ	י	ן
ה	ר	ח	מ	ן	שׁ	ב	ת
מ	נ	ח	ה	נ	שׁ	מ	ה
כ	ל	ה	צ	י	צ	י	ת

VOCABULARY CHALLENGE

You know the English meaning of many of the words in the Word Find activity above. Read the Hebrew and give the English meaning for the words you know.

77

BE ALERT

Following are the definitions of each word in this exercise.

two – שְׁנַיִם
Haman – הָמָן
hear – שְׁמַע
the merciful one – הָרַחֲמָן
Abraham – אַבְרָהָם
knees – בִּרְכַּיִם
to life – לְחַיִּים
days – יָמִים
commandment – מִצְוָה
minyan; quorum for public prayer – מִנְיָן
man – אָדָם
Egypt – מִצְרַיִם

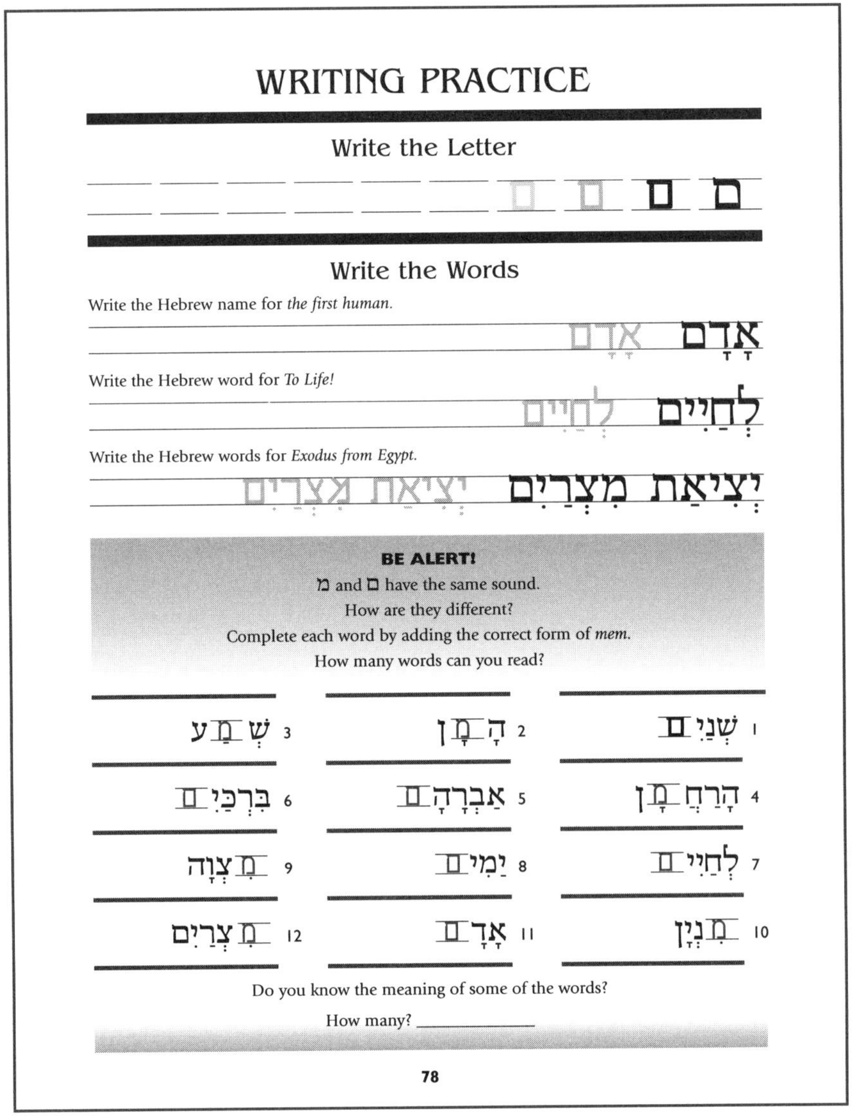

WRITING PRACTICE

Write the Letter

ם ם ם ם

Write the Words

Write the Hebrew name for *the first human.*

אָדָם אָדָם

Write the Hebrew word for *To Life!*

לְחַיִּים לְחַיִּים

Write the Hebrew words for *Exodus from Egypt.*

יְצִיאַת מִצְרַיִם יְצִיאַת מִצְרַיִם

BE ALERT!

מ and ם have the same sound.
How are they different?
Complete each word by adding the correct form of *mem.*
How many words can you read?

3 שְׁ__ַע	2 הָ__ָן	1 שְׁנַיִ__
6 בִּרְכַּיִ__	5 אַבְרָהָ__	4 הָרַחֲ__ָן
9 __ִצְוָה	8 יָמִי__	7 לְחַיִּי__
12 __ִצְרַיִם	11 אָדָ__	10 __ִנְיָן

Do you know the meaning of some of the words?

How many? ____________

78

USING THE PHOTOGRAPH

What occasion do you think this couple is celebrating? Does it have to be something Jewish? [**e.g., birthday, anniversary, holiday**]

THE LIVING TRADITION

Play the song "To Life – *l'ḥayyim*" from the movie *Fiddler on the Roof*. Have the students count the number of times the phrase "to life" is sung and the number of times the word *l'ḥayyim* is sung.

How do the students feel when they hear this song? Why do you think the expression "to life" is used? [**Judaism believes that we are supposed to enjoy life. Depriving oneself of the joys of life, as is done in some religions, is frowned upon in Judaism.**]

Emphasize that this expression is used on joyous occasions. Judaism has always placed a priority on life, and this expression verbalizes that feeling.

WORD POWER

In addition to circling the appropriate word on each line, have the students put a square around all the other words that have been taught as key words in this book.

ḥallah; braided braid – חַלָה
havdalah; separation – הַבְדָלָה
helper – שַׁמָשׁ
commandment – מִצְוָה
prophet – נָבִיא

THE LIVING TRADITION לְחַיִּים

לְחַיִּים means "to life." At a special celebration, such as a wedding or graduation, it is traditional to clink our glasses together and say לְחַיִּים.

The word חַיִּים means "life" and appears in many of our prayers.

WORD POWER

Read aloud the Hebrew words in each line. Circle the word that has the same meaning as the English in the box.

שֶׁמֶשׁ	הַבְדָלָה	חַלָה	(בְּרָכָה)	blessing	1
(לְחַיִּים)	עֲבָדִים	חָכָם	מִצְוָה	to life	2
שְׁתַּיִם	(שְׁמַע)	בָּנִים	נָבִיא	hear	3
יְצִיאַת	עַיִן	(עֲלִיָה)	מִצְרַיִם	going up	4
יְשִׁיבָה	(צְדָקָה)	שָׁמַיִם	יְלָדִים	justice	5

CHECKPOINT

Choose from the following techniques:

1. Call on students to read the word in each box and provide the meaning if it has been learned.

2. Call out a box number at random and have a student read the word in that box.

3. Call out a Hebrew letter that has been learned and have students read all the words in the grid that contain that letter.

4. Call out the English meaning of a word and have the students call out the box number with its corresponding Hebrew word.

5. A word that means "a righteous person" is a _____.

6. A word that is really a phrase is _____.

7. The name of our special language is_____.

FYI

Basic Checkpoint Technique

Use the Checkpoint to assess each student's progress. Listen to students read individually. Circle errors lightly in pencil in their textbooks. Reteach problem letters and retest students, erasing the pencil marks when they read the word correctly.

AN *ALEF-BET* CHART

Have the students color in the appropriate letters on page 160.

CHECKPOINT
Read the Hebrew word in each box.

צַדִּיק 4	נָבִיא 3	רַבִּי 2	אִמָּא 1
לְחַיִּים 8	אָחִי 7	דָּוִד 6	יְהִי 5
מִצְוָה 12	עֲלִיָּה 11	לְכִי 10	כִּי 9
צִיצִית 16	עִבְרִית 15	נִין 14	אֲנִי 13
הַתִּקְוָה 20	שִׁירָה 19	בְּרִית 18	תְּקִיעָה 17

Which box contains the boy's name *David*?

AN *ALEF BET* CHART
You have learned six new letters in Lessons 9-13:
ע נ ן ח י ם.
Turn to the *Alef Bet* Chart on page 160. Color in the new letters.
Can you say the name and sound of each letter you now know?

80

LESSON 14

Pages: 81–85
Key Word: תּוֹרָה
New Vowels: וֹ ֹ
Alef-Bet Flashcards: 29, 30
Word Cards: 31, 32, 33, 34, 35, 36

REVIEW EXERCISE

Using the chalkboard or flannelboard, review the seven letters used in line 1 on page 81 (without the vowel). Review the vowels learned so far by placing each one in turn with each letter. Have students take turns reading the sounds.

KEY WORD (תּוֹרָה)

Ask what the picture is at the beginning of the lesson. How do you feel when you see the Torah? Why do we regularly read the Torah out loud in the synagogue? **[so that everyone has the opportunity to hear it and so that its stories and laws will not be forgotten]**

Sing the song *Torah Tzivah Lanu Moshe.*

INTRODUCE THE NEW VOWELS –
(*HOLAM:* וֹ ֹ)

Using *alef-bet* flashcards #29 and #30, show the new vowel *holam* to students. Then add the *alef-bet* flashcards for the other vowels learned, review, and drill them. (5, 6, 13, 16, 21, 22) Display and read word card #31 (תּוֹרָה). Have the students identify each letter and vowel.

READING PRACTICE

Call on students at random to read lines 1–3.

NOW READ & READ AGAIN

Call on students randomly to read each line. Don't forget to recycle the exercise!

HERITAGE WORDS

How do we greet each other on Shabbat? [שַׁבָּת שָׁלוֹם]

What is the difference between the *ḥallah* we use on Shabbat and the one we make for רֹאשׁ הַשָּׁנָה? **[On Shabbat it is braided and on Rosh Hashanah it is round.]** Is the blessing the same? **[Yes]** Can you recite the blessing recited over bread? What does it mean? **[Praised are You, *Adonai* our God, Ruler of the universe, who brings forth bread from the earth.]** הַמּוֹצִיא literally means "the one who brings forth."

What do we do to show that the Torah is a holy object? **[dress it with ornaments, kiss it, keep it in Ark with Eternal Light, stand when the ark is open, etc.]**

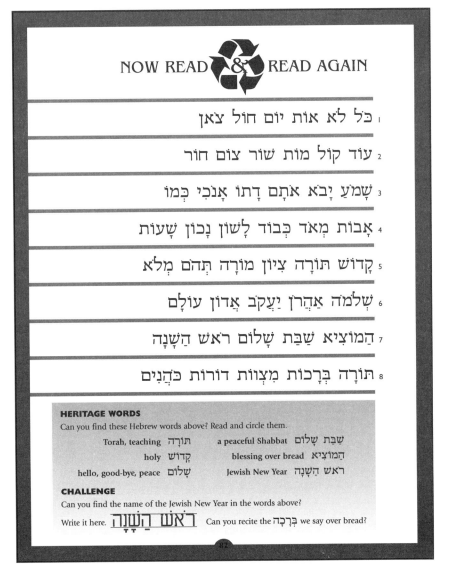

NOW READ & READ AGAIN

1. כֹּל לֹא אוֹת יוֹם חוֹל צֹאן

2. עוֹד קוֹל מוֹת שׁוֹר צוֹם חוֹר

3. שָׁמַע יָבֹא אַתָּם דָּתוֹ אָנֹכִי כְּמוֹ

4. אָבוֹת מְאֹד כְּבוֹד לָשׁוֹן נָכוֹן שָׁעוֹת

5. קָדוֹשׁ תּוֹרָה צִיּוֹן מוֹרָה תְּהֹם מְלֹא

6. שְׁלֹמֹה אַהֲרֹן יַעֲקֹב אֲדוֹן עוֹלָם

7. הַמּוֹצִיא שַׁבָּת שָׁלוֹם רֹאשׁ הַשָּׁנָה

8. תּוֹרָה בְּרָכוֹת מִצְווֹת דּוֹרוֹת כֹּהֲנִים

HERITAGE WORDS

Can you find these Hebrew words above? Read and circle them.

Torah, teaching	תּוֹרָה	a peaceful Shabbat	שַׁבָּת שָׁלוֹם
holy	קָדוֹשׁ	blessing over bread	הַמּוֹצִיא
hello, good-bye, peace	שָׁלוֹם	Jewish New Year	רֹאשׁ הַשָּׁנָה

CHALLENGE

Can you find the name of the Jewish New Year in the words above?

Write it here. רֹאשׁ הַשָּׁנָה Can you recite the בְּרָכָה we say over bread?

82

WORD FIND

Have the students complete this exercise independently.

WORD RIDDLE

Answer: שָׁלוֹם

WORD FIND
Read aloud the Hebrew word in each box.

Find the Hebrew word in the chain of letters and circle it.

עוֹלָהְעַלְעוֹלָם(שָׁלוֹה)הֶם	עוֹלָם	1
מַיִםמַ(מִנְדָהְיַיְ(מִנְיָן)	מִנְיָן	2
עַל(עֲלִיָה)הַלְיָהְעוֹלָהָת	עֲלִיָה	3
כֵּנָהְוּנָהַ(כַּוָנָה)זֶכָּהֶ	כַּוָנָה	4
שָׁלוֹהְלוֹםשָׁלוֹשַׁהְ(שָׁלוֹם)	שָׁלוֹם	5
נְשָׁמְאָטְמַהְ(נְשָׁמָה)שָׁנָמָה	נְשָׁמָה	6
רֹ(שַׁחֲרִית)חֲרִיָהַשַׁחֲרַת	שַׁחֲרִית	7
תּוֹדָהְמוֹרָהֹ(תּוֹרָה)דֹוּתֹוֹה	תּוֹרָה	8
כְּרִיתְרִיתַבְרִי(בְּרִית)הַרִית	בְּרִית	9
מִשְׁעַשְׁעָ(אְשְׁמַע)שֶׁמַצְמַעַשׁ	שְׁמַע	10

WORD RIDDLE
My name means "peace." My name also means "hello" and "good-bye."

My name contains the vowel וֹ. Who am I?

83

WRITE THE WORDS

Choose six students to come to the chalkboard with their books and have each write one of the words two times. The rest of the class should complete the exercise in the book.

RHYME TIME

Have the students complete this exercise independently. Then call on students to read aloud each of the rhyming sets. Call on another student to read the word on each line that did not rhyme and have that student come to the chalkboard and write the word.

WORD RIDDLE

Answer: קָדוֹשׁ

WRITING PRACTICE

Write the Words

Write the Hebrew word for *a peaceful Shabbat.*

שַׁבָּת שָׁלוֹם

Write the Hebrew word for *the blessing over bread.*

הַמּוֹצִיא

Write the Hebrew words for *the Jewish New Year.*

רֹאשׁ הַשָּׁנָה

Write the Hebrew word for *Torah.*

תּוֹרָה

Write the Hebrew word for *holy.*

קָדוֹשׁ

Write the Hebrew word for *hello, good-bye, peace.*

שָׁלוֹם

RHYME TIME

Read aloud the words on each line. Three words rhyme. Circle the word that does not rhyme. Now read aloud the rhyming words. Write the words you circled.

WORD RIDDLE

I am a word repeated three times in a row when we recite the עֲמִידָה. I mean "holy, holy, holy." I begin with the letter ק. Who am I?

בַּת

1. בַּר   קַר   הַר   (בַּת)
2. שׁוֹר   (חוֹם)   חוֹר   תּוֹר
3. תּוֹרָה   (לִקְרֹא)   אוֹרָה   מוֹרָה
4. לָשׁוֹן   שָׁעוֹן   (עוֹלָם)   נָכוֹן
5. קָדוֹשׁ   רֹאשׁ   שָׁלוֹשׁ   (רוֹצָה)
6. (דוֹר)   חוֹל   אֶתְמוֹל   הַכֹּל
7. (אוֹתוֹ)   חַיּוֹת   שָׁנוֹת   בְּרִיּוֹת
8. שָׁלוֹם   אָדֹם   (חַלּוֹת)   חֲלוֹם

84

USING THE PHOTOGRAPH

- What Jewish objects do you see in the photograph? [*kippah*, Torah, *tallit*, *yad*, *magen david* – Jewish star, *menorah*, etc.]
- Why do we use a *yad* – pointer – when reading from the Torah? [**so we do not smudge the letters in the Torah with our fingers and make the Torah dirty**]

THE LIVING TRADITION

In addition to being the name of our holiest book, "Torah" also means "teaching." Why is the word for "teaching" used as the name for the Jewish people's holiest document and object? [**The words in the Torah scroll teach us about the history of the Jewish people, as well as teaching us how to live a Jewish life.**]

Ask students to draw a picture depicting their favorite story or scene from the Torah and to explain why they chose it. Have the students write the word תּוֹרָה on their pictures.

CONNECTIONS

Have the students complete this exercise independently. Then call on one student to read the opening word-part and another student to read the concluding word-part.

Another option is to play a matching game. Distribute cards with the beginning of the word to some students and cards with the ending of the word to the other students. Students find a match for their part of the word. At the end of the game, everyone should be standing in pairs.

THE LIVING TRADITION תּוֹרָה

The word תּוֹרָה means "teaching" and is the name of the Five Books of Moses. The תּוֹרָה teaches us how to live good and honest lives. The stories in the תּוֹרָה tell us about our ancestors Abraham and Sarah, Isaac and Rebecca, Jacob, Leah, and Rachel. We read portions of the תּוֹרָה each week in the synagogue to help us remember God's teachings.

CONNECTIONS

Read the words in each column.

Connect the beginning of a phrase in column א with its ending in column ב. Read each completed phrase aloud.

85

LESSON 15

Pages: 86–91
Key Word: טַלִית
New Letter: ט
Alef-Bet Flashcard: 31
Word Cards: 37, 38, 39

REVIEW EXERCISE

Tic-Tac-Toe

Play "tic-tac-toe" as described in #4 on page viii. Use flashcards #1–30.

KEY WORD (טַלִית)

Have the students look at the picture of the Key word and then identify it. What sound does the first letter have? **[t]**

When is the *tallit* worn? **[during morning services. It is worn every day, including Shabbat and holidays.]** When is the only time a *tallit* is worn at night? **[Kol Nidrei service on Yom Kippur eve]**

INTRODUCE THE NEW LETTER – ט

Display word card #37 (טַלִית) and teach the letter *tet*. Have one of the teams identify each of the letters in the word. Did anyone identify the *tet* as being a *mem*? This is a common error.

What letter has the same sound as the *tet*? **[tav]** What other letters in the Hebrew alphabet have the same sound? **[ח=א, ע=ב, ו=כ, כ]**

Since *mem* and *tet* are often confused, point to the *mem* on the *alef-bet* chart, have the students identify it, and ask the students to describe the difference in appearance between the *mem* and *tet*. A helpful hint for the students is that "*mem* has a man standing on a mountain (מ); *tet* is open on the top (ט)."

READING PRACTICE

Return to the tic-tac-toe game and have students from each team read each of the three lines, with their teamates repeating in unison.

NOW READ & READ AGAIN

Continue the tic-tac-toe game and have students from each team alternate reading the lines of reading practice. Correct reading of a line allows that team to place a letter on the tic-tac-toe board. To give more students a chance to read, have each student read only two or three words at a time.

HERITAGE WORDS

יוֹם טוֹב literally means "good day". Why do you think this phrase is used for holiday or festival?

Do you know any other Rosh Hashanah greetings beside שָׁנָה טוֹבָה?

1 טוֹן טִיב מָט אַט חַיְט מוֹטוֹ

2 טוֹב טַל אִטִי טָרִי שׁוֹט קָט

3 מְטָה מוֹט קָטָן חִטָה שָׁחַט לָטַשׁ

4 לְאַט מָטָר חָטָא מְעַט שָׁבָט בָּטַח

5 טַלִית טָהוֹר אָטָד טַעַם טִבְעִי טָמַן

6 קְטַנָה עֲטָרָה מִקְלָט חֲטָאִים הַבִּיטָה

7 שְׁבָטִים טוֹבִים בִּטָחוֹן נְטִילַת יָדַיִם

8 טַלִית שָׁנָה טוֹבָה יוֹם טוֹב

HERITAGE WORDS
Can you find these Hebrew words above? Read and circle them.

טַלִית — *tallit*, prayer shawl
יוֹם טוֹב — holiday, festival
שָׁנָה טוֹבָה — Happy New Year

CHALLENGE
Can you find the Hebrew phrase we say at רֹאשׁ הַשָׁנָה to wish each other *a good year*?

SOUNDS LIKE

Have the students complete the exercise independently. When everyone has finished, call on students to read each line aloud and provide their answer.

Another option is for the teacher to read each line and have the students circle the sound-alike words.

WORD WIZARD

After the students have completed this exercise, have them create their own Word Wizard using the Key or Heritage words from each lesson. Take word cards #1-39 and distribute them randomly to the students, who must create a Word Wizard exercise for the card they receive. Then have the students exchange papers and have them complete their classmates' puzzle.

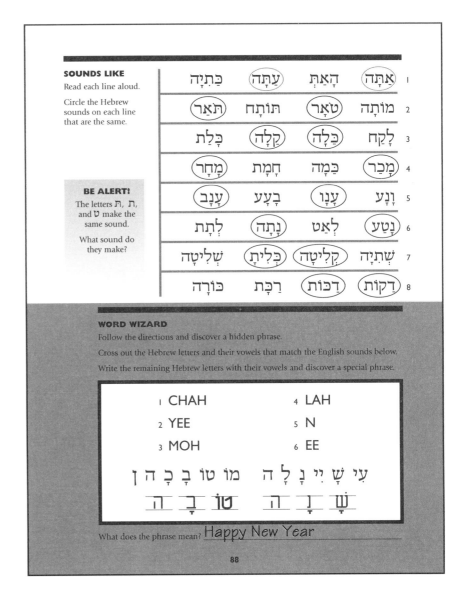

SOUNDS LIKE

Read each line aloud.

Circle the Hebrew sounds on each line that are the same.

כָּתְיָה	(עַתָּה)	(עָתָּה)	הָאַתְּ	(אַתָּה) 1
(תֹּאַר)	תּוֹתֵחַ	(טֹאַר)	מוֹתָה	2
כָּלַת	(קָלָה)	(כָּלָה)	לָקַח	3
(מְכַר)	חָמְתָ	כַּמָּה	(מְכַר)	4
(עָנָב)	בָּעַע	(עָנוּ)	וְנַע	5
לְתָת	(נָתָה)	לָאַט	(נָטַע)	6
שְׁלִיטָה	(קְלִיתָ)	(קְלִיטָה)	שְׁתִיָּה	7
כּוֹרָה	רַכַּת	(דַּכּוֹת)	(דְּקוֹת)	8

BE ALERT!

The letters ת, ט, and ט make the same sound.

What sound do they make?

WORD WIZARD

Follow the directions and discover a hidden phrase.

Cross out the Hebrew letters and their vowels that match the English sounds below.

Write the remaining Hebrew letters with their vowels and discover a special phrase.

1 CHAH	4 LAH
2 YEE	5 N
3 MOH	6 EE

עִי שָׁ יִי נָ לָ ה   מוֹ טוֹ בָ כָ ה ן

שָׁ‌ נָ‌ ה   טוֹ‌ בָ‌ ה

What does the phrase mean? _Happy New Year_

88

WRITING THE LETTER

If you are teaching print writing, after demonstrating the method for writing the letter *tet* you should also review how to write the letter *mem* to illustrate the differences, since the two letters are sometimes confused.

SEARCH AND CIRCLE

Have the students complete this exercise independently.

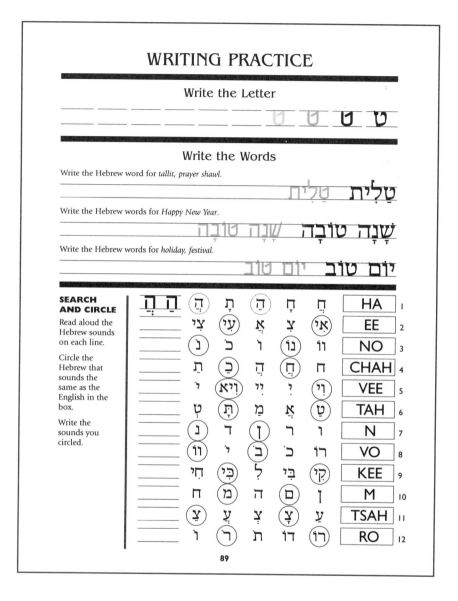

USING THE PHOTOGRAPH

- What do you think is the occasion of this photograph? **[bar mitzvah]**
- What do you think the rabbi is saying to the boy?

THE LIVING TRADITION

Bring a *tallit* to class and allow the students to hold it and feel the fringes, the *tzitzit*. What is the significance of the *tzitzit*? **[They remind us of God's commandments. As it says in the third paragraph of the Shema, "...in every generation they shall put fringes on the corners of their garments...Looking upon it you will be reminded of all the *mitzvot* of Adonai..."]**

How do they feel when they touch the *tallit*? Explain that there are special rules for tying the *tzitzit* so that even though different *tallitot* may look very different, the one thing that will always be the same is the way in which the *tzitzit* are tied. Make sure the students can differentiate between the *tzitzit* on the four corners of the *tallit* and the decorative fringes that may be along the edge of the *tallit*.

MIX AND MATCH

Have the students complete this exercise independently.

THE LIVING TRADITION טַלִית

טַלִית is the Hebrew word for "prayer shawl." Many Jewish adults wear a טַלִית during morning prayer services. The four corners of the טַלִית have knotted fringes called צִיצִית. The תּוֹרָה tells us to look at the צִיצִית so that we will remember to follow God's commandments.

MIX AND MATCH

Connect each Hebrew word with its English meaning. Read each Hebrew-English match aloud.

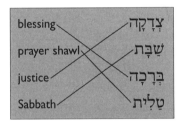

blessing — צְדָקָה
prayer shawl — שַׁבָּת
justice — בְּרָכָה
Sabbath — טַלִית

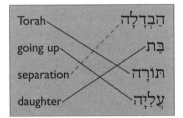

Torah — הַבְדָלָה
going up — בַּת
separation — תּוֹרָה
daughter — עֲלִיָה

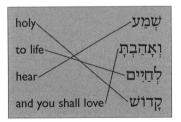

holy — שְׁמַע
to life — וְאָהַבְתָּ
hear — לְחַיִּים
and you shall love — קָדוֹשׁ

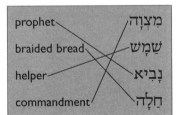

prophet — מִצְוָה
braided bread — שַׁמָּשׁ
helper — נָבִיא
commandment — חַלָּה

90

CHECKPOINT

Choose from the following techniques:

1. Call on students to read the word in each box and provide the meaning if it has been learned.

2. Call out a box number at random and have a student read the word in that box.

3. Call out a Hebrew letter that has been learned and have students read all the words in the grid that contain that letter.

4. Call on students to read all the words that rhyme with each other. **[1–6, 4–18, 7–17, 9–11, 9–19, 11–19, 12–16, 14–20]**

5. Call on students to read all words that conclude with a special final letter. **[9, 10, 11, 12, 15, 16, 19]**

FYI

Basic Checkpoint Technique

Use the Checkpoint to assess each student's progress. Listen to students read individually. Circle errors lightly in pencil in their textbooks. Reteach problem letters and retest students, erasing the pencil marks when they read the word correctly.

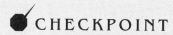

CHECKPOINT
Practice reading the words.

קָדוֹשׁ 4	כָּבוֹד 3	רִבּוֹנוּ 2	אוֹת 1
טוֹב 8	חוֹל 7	מִצְווֹת 6	טָהוֹר 5
שָׁלוֹם 12	נָכוֹן 11	כֹּהֲנִים 10	צִיּוֹן 9
צוֹם 16	עוֹלָם 15	נוֹרָא 14	הַמּוֹצִיא 13
תּוֹרָה 20	לָשׁוֹן 19	רֹאשׁ 18	קוֹל 17

91

LESSON 16

Pages: 92–96
Key Word: אֱמֶת
New Vowels: ֶ ֱ
Alef-Bet Flashcards: 32, 33
Word Cards: 40, 41, 42, 43

KEY WORD (אֱמֶת)

Print אֱמֶת on the chalkboard and ask for a volunteer to identify each of the letters. Read the word aloud and ask the students what sound they think this vowel makes. Define the word for the students. *Emet* means truth. People must speak *emet* when dealing with one another. *Emet* is also part of the nature of God. That is to say, God represents truth.

Are there times when it would be acceptable not to tell the truth?

What is a "white lie"? Is it acceptable to tell "white lies"? [**Our tradition does not consider it wrong to tell a "white lie." For example, it is permitted to tell a lie in order to avoid strife and contention. Of course, common sense must be a guiding principle.**]

INTRODUCE THE NEW VOWEL – (*SEGOL:* ֶ and *ḤATAF SEGOL:* ֱ)

Display *alef-bet* flashcard #32 (ֶ) and introduce this vowel and its sound. Hold *alef-bet* flashcards #13 (ֵ) and #21 (ִ) next to the *segol* and ask how the *segol* differs in sound and appearance.

Display *alef-bet* flash card #33 (ֱ) and ask what two vowels are seen here. [*segol* **and** *shvah*] What other vowel also contains "two vowels in one?" [*ḥataf pataḥ*] Explain that just as in the case of the *ḥataf pataḥ*, the *shvah* does not change the pronunciation of the primary vowel.

READING PRACTICE

Read line 1 for the class and have them repeat the line in unison. Call on a student to read line 2 and then have the entire class repeat in unison. Repeat this procedure with line 3.

NOW READ & READ AGAIN

Have one student read a line and then call out another line number for the next student to read.

HERITAGE WORDS

What object do we keep in the אֲרוֹן הַקֹּדֶשׁ? [Torah]

In what blessing do we recite the phrase הַמּוֹצִיא לֶחֶם? [the blessing over bread]

Why do you think that a drawing of the tablets of the Ten Commandments was chosen to represent the word אֱמֶת – at the top of the previous page? [You shall not lie is one of the Ten Commandments; the Ten Commandments are from God and God represents truth, etc.]

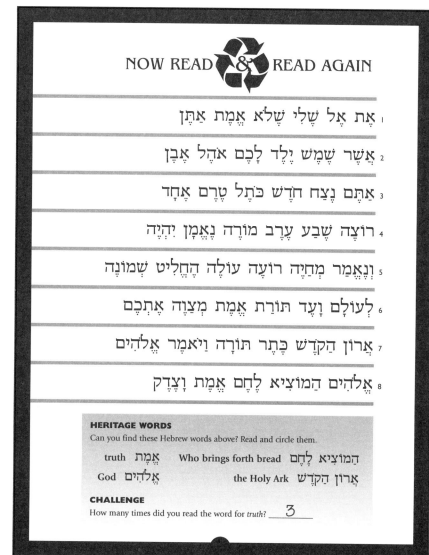

NOW READ & READ AGAIN

1. אֶת אֵל שֶׁלִּי שֶׁלֹּא אֱמֶת אַתֶּן

2. אֲשֶׁר שֶׁמֶשׁ יֶלֶד לָכֶם אֹהֶל אֶבֶן

3. אַתֶּם נֶצַח חֹדֶשׁ כֹּתֶל טֶרֶם אֶחָד

4. רוֹצָה שֶׁבַע עֶרֶב מוֹרֶה נֶאֱמָן יִהְיֶה

5. וְנֶאֱמַר מְחַיֶּה רוֹעֶה עוֹלֶה הֶחֱלִיט שְׁמוֹנֶה

6. לְעוֹלָם וָעֶד תּוֹרַת אֱמֶת מְצַוֶּה אֶתְכֶם

7. אֲרוֹן הַקֹּדֶשׁ כֶּתֶר תּוֹרָה וַיֹּאמֶר אֱלֹהִים

8. אֱלֹהִים הַמּוֹצִיא לֶחֶם אֱמֶת וָצֶדֶק

HERITAGE WORDS

Can you find these Hebrew words above? Read and circle them.

truth אֱמֶת   Who brings forth bread הַמּוֹצִיא לֶחֶם

God אֱלֹהִים   the Holy Ark אֲרוֹן הַקֹּדֶשׁ

CHALLENGE

How many times did you read the word for *truth*? ___3___

BE ALERT

Following the format of the example given at the top of the page,
מֹשֶׁה = מֹשֶׁה, call on students to come to the chalkboard and diagram
the five words containing a *shin* whose dot serves two purposes.

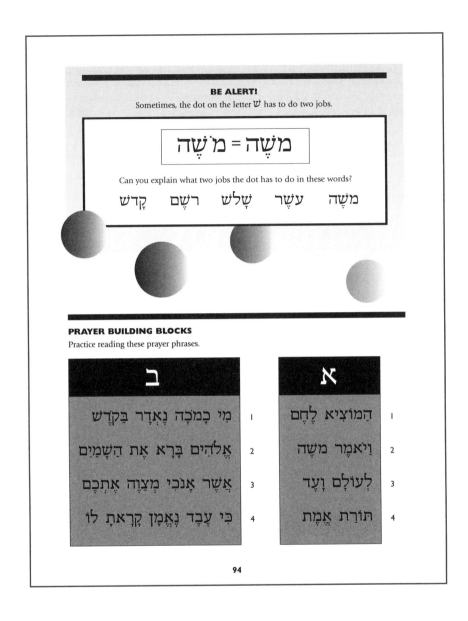

SEARCH AND CIRCLE

Read the instructions and have the students complete this exercise independently.

WRITING PRACTICE

Shalom Uvrachah [the student's edition] is available in two versions—one for teaching print writing and one for teaching script. As you know, this universal Teacher's Edition can be used with either version. You can see samples of every letter in script format on page xiv.

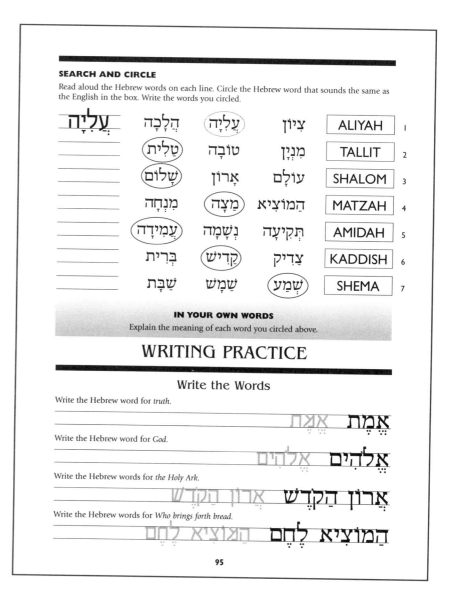

USING THE PHOTOGRAPH

- What is the relationship between the two girls? **[friends, sisters, or cousins]**
- How do you think one of the girls would feel if she found out that her friend/sister had lied to her? **[angry, sad, disappointed, etc.]**

THE LIVING TRADITION

There is a statement found in *Pirkei Avot* (Ethics of the Fathers) which reads: "The world rests on three pillars: truth – אֱמֶת, justice – צֶדֶק, and peace – שָׁלוֹם. Write each pillar on a sign (in Hebrew) and place each sign in a corner of the classroom. Ask the students which of these three they feel is the most important and tell them to stand by that sign. Have the students discuss the reason for their choice. At the end, explain that the Rabbis thought that all three were equally important because the absence of any one of them threatens a society's survival.

NAME KNOW-HOW

Each Hebrew name represents a biblical figure. Ask if the students can identify any of the people.

Moses – led the Israelites out of Egypt
Benjamin – youngest son of Jacob
Adam – first human being
David – second King of Israel
Miriam – Moses' sister
Rebecca – Isaac's wife
Hannah – Mother of the prophet Samuel
Deborah – prophet

THE LIVING TRADITION אֱמֶת

The Hebrew word אֱמֶת means "truth." In our prayers we say that God's words are true and righteous: אֱמֶת וְצֶדֶק. In the Ten Commandments we are told to tell the truth—אֱמֶת. We are also taught that relationships between people must be built on אֱמֶת, on trust and truth.

NAME KNOW-HOW

Match each Hebrew name with its translation. Read each match aloud.

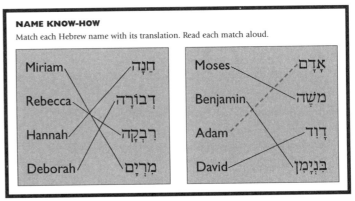

LESSON 17

Pages: 97–102
Key Word: פֶּסַח
New Letters: פ ס
Alef-Bet Flashcards: 34, 35
Word Cards: 44, 45, 46, 47

REVIEW EXERCISE

Distribute *alef-bet* flashcards #1–34 randomly to students. Class size will determine how many cards each student receives. Tell the students in advance that one of the cards being distributed is the new letter to be learned in this lesson.

Call out the name or sound of a letter or vowel and ask the student with that card to hold it up as it is called. Consider calling out letter/vowel combinations to add complexity to this exercise. For example, when calling the word *shemen*, the students with the *shin, mem, final nun, segol,* and *ḥataf segol* cards would all display them.

KEY WORD (פֶּסַח)

Ask the students what the Hebrew name is for the holiday of Passover. What does *Pesaḥ* mean? **[pass over]** Why does the holiday have this name? **[The angel of death passed over the Israelite homes when God delivered the last plague – the killing of the firstborn.]**

"My favorite part of the *Pesaḥ* seder is _____."

INTRODUCE THE NEW LETTER – פ

Point to the *pay* on the *alef-bet* chart and ask the student who has the flashcard with this letter to display it. Teach the letter *pay* and its sound. Give special attention to making sure the students can differentiate between the letters *pay, bet, tav, shin, mem, kaf,* and *tet.*

Have the students point to the *pay* in the word *Pesaḥ* in their textbooks.

READING PRACTICE

Randomly call on students to read each of these three lines. Remember, these lines can be repeated to give more students a chance to read.

NOW READ & READ AGAIN

Have students work in pairs reading lines to each other. Match a stronger reader with a weaker reader. Listen as they practice, and correct errors that you hear.

HERITAGE WORDS

Why do many Jews wear a כִּפָּה? **[shows our respect for God; shows we are proud to be Jewish]**

How many people are in your מִשְׁפָּחָה?

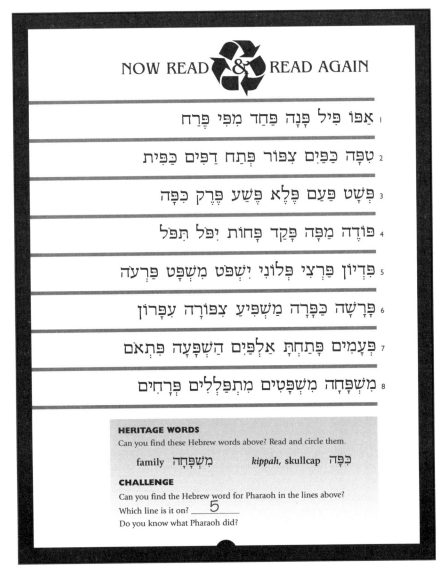

NOW READ & READ AGAIN

1 אַפּוֹ פִּיל פָּנָה פַּחַד מִפִּי פֶּרַח

2 טִפָּה כַּפַּים צִפּוֹר פָּתַח דַפִּים כַּפִּית

3 פְּשַׁט פַּעַם מְלֵא פֶּשַׁע פֶּרֶק כַּפָּה

4 פּוֹדֶה מַפָּה פָּקַד פָּחוֹת יִפֹּל תִּפֹּל

5 פִּדְיוֹן פַּרְצִי פְּלוֹנִי יִשְׁפֹּט מִשְׁפָּט פַּרְעֹה

6 פָּרָשָׁה כַּפָּרָה מַשְׁפִּיעַ צִפּוֹרָה עֶפְרוֹן

7 פְּעָמִים פָּתַחְתָּ אֲלָפִים הַשְׁפָּעָה פִּתְאֹם

8 מִשְׁפָּחָה מִשְׁפָּטִים מִתְפַּלְלִים פְּרָחִים

HERITAGE WORDS

Can you find these Hebrew words above? Read and circle them.

family מִשְׁפָּחָה   *kippah*, skullcap כִּפָּה

CHALLENGE

Can you find the Hebrew word for Pharaoh in the lines above?

Which line is it on? ____5____

Do you know what Pharaoh did?

RHYME TIME

Have the students complete this exercise independently. Then call on a student to read aloud each of the rhyming sets. Call on another student to read the words on each line that did not rhyme.

Another option is to call on students to come to the chalkboard and write the two words that rhyme. Then have them explain which part of the words are the rhyming sections.

INTRODUCE THE NEW LETTER – ס

Display *alef-bet* flashcard #28 (ם) and ask the students to identify its name and sound. Hold up *alef-bet* flashcard #35 (ס) next to it and have the students describe how the two letters differ. Then teach the *samech's* name and sound. Emphasize that the *samech* is not a final letter.

READING PRACTICE

Read the first line and have the students respond in unison. Call on students to first read line 2 or 3 and to then repeat it singing the sounds to a simple tune.

Ask for a volunteer to read the Key word and to name each of the letters.

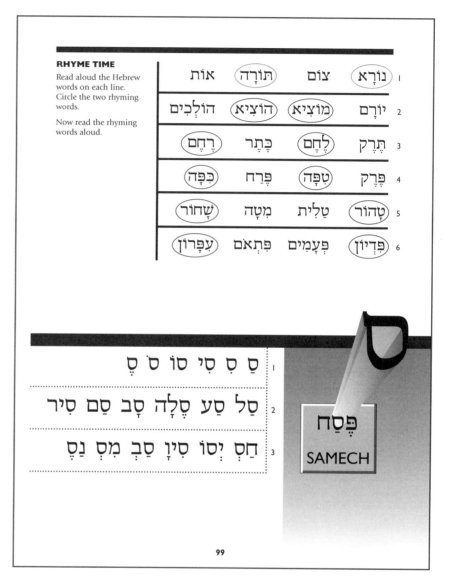

RHYME TIME
Read aloud the Hebrew words on each line. Circle the two rhyming words.

Now read the rhyming words aloud.

אוֹת	(תּוֹרָה)	צוֹם	(נוֹרָא)		1
הוֹלְכִים	(הוֹצִיא)	(מוֹצִיא)	יוֹרֶם		2
(רֶחֶם)	כֶּתֶר	(לֶחֶם)	תֶּרֶק		3
(כַּפָּה)	פֶּרַח	(טִפָּה)	פֶּרֶק		4
(שָׁחוֹר)	מִטָּה	טַלִּית	(טָהוֹר)		5
(עֶפְרוֹן)	פִּתְאֹם	פְּעָמִים	(פִּדְיוֹן)		6

סַ סָ סִי סוֹ סֹ סֶ ₁

סַל סַע סְלָה סָב סַם סִיר ₂

חַס יְסוֹ סִין סַב מְסָ נֵס ₃

פֶּסַח
SAMECH

99

LESSON SEVENTEEN

99

NOW READ & READ AGAIN

Number eight slips of paper 1 through 8 and put them in a small bag. When it is each student's turn to read, the student picks a slip of paper out of the bag and reads the line corresponding to the number on the slip. Make sure to recycle the exercise in order to provide reading practice to as many students as possible.

HERITAGE WORDS

What do we do during the *Pesaḥ* seder that shows our חֶסֶד for the Egyptians who enslaved our people? **[take out drops of wine when we recite the ten plagues to show that we cannot be truly happy since people had to suffer and die so that we could be free]**

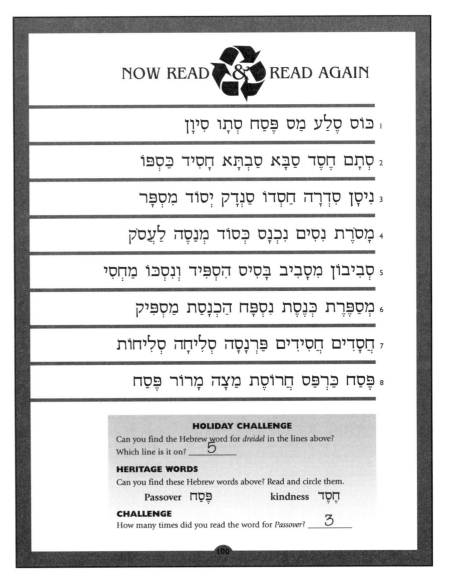

NOW READ & READ AGAIN

1 כּוֹס סֶלַע מַס פֶּסַח סְתָו סִיוָן

2 סְתָם חֶסֶד סַבָּא סַבְתָּא חָסִיד כַּסְפּוֹ

3 נִיסָן סְדְרָה חַסְדוֹ סַנְדָּק יְסוֹד מִסְפָּר

4 מָסֹרֶת נִסִּים נִכְנָס כְּסוֹד מְנַסֶּה לַעֲסֹק

5 סְבִיבוֹן מִסָּבִיב בָּסִיס הִסְפִּיד וְנִסְכּוֹ מַחְסִי

6 מִסְפֶּרֶת כְּנֶסֶת נִסְפַּח הַכְּנֶסֶת מַסְפִּיק

7 חֲסָדִים חֲסִידִים פַּרְנָסָה סְלִיחָה סְלִיחוֹת

8 פֶּסַח כַּרְפַּס חֲרוֹסֶת מַצָּה מָרוֹר פֶּסַח

HOLIDAY CHALLENGE

Can you find the Hebrew word for *dreidel* in the lines above? Which line is it on? ___5___

HERITAGE WORDS

Can you find these Hebrew words above? Read and circle them.

Passover פֶּסַח   kindness חֶסֶד

CHALLENGE

How many times did you read the word for *Passover*? ___3___

100

LESSON SEVENTEEN

100

WRITE THE LETTERS

Have the students complete the writing practice exercises as in previous lessons. Ensure that the students are not making the *samech* too similarly to a final *mem*.

WORD FIND

Read the instructions and have the students complete this exercise independently. While reviewing, ask students to give the English meaning for each word they find.

1. matzah
2. Passover
3. truth
4. kindness
5. dreidel (this word has not been formally taught)
6. Torah
7. family

USING THE PHOTOGRAPH

Identify the seder objects on the table. **[matzah, *haggadah*, Kiddush cups, Elijah's cup, seder plate, etc.]**

THE LIVING TRADITION

While we are no longer slaves in the traditional sense, are there things in today's society to which we are enslaved? Make a list on the chalkboard and discuss how we can free ourselves from being slaves to these things. Help the students to think about the enslaving nature of things such as money, power, technology etc.

How does Judaism help guide us and keep us focused on what is truly important? **[observing *mitzvot*, learning from our history, etc.]**

THE LIVING TRADITION פֶּסַח

When our people were slaves in Egypt, God sent מֹשֶׁה to lead us out of Egypt to freedom. We celebrate this event each spring with the festival of פֶּסַח. Every year we retell the פֶּסַח story when we read the *haggadah*.

THE פֶּסַח SEDER

Read each Hebrew word and its English meaning aloud. Read each sentence describing a פֶּסַח food. Write the correct Hebrew word to answer each question.

מָרוֹר	מַצָּה	חֲרוֹסֶת	כַּרְפַּס	יַיִן
bitter herbs	matzah	chopped apples and nuts *ḥaroset*	greens	wine

1. Everyone was in a hurry to leave Egypt and did not have time to wait for the bread dough to rise. My dough hardened into a flat, crunchy kind of bread.

   Who am I? __מַצָּה__

2. I am the greens on the seder plate. I represent springtime and new life. I am dipped into salt water to remind us of the tears we cried when we were slaves.

   Who am I? __כַּרְפַּס__

3. I taste bitter. I am a reminder of our bitter lives as slaves. Who am I? __מָרוֹר__

4. I remind everyone of the bricks we had to make when we were slaves in Egypt.

   Who am I? __חֲרוֹסֶת__

5. I am a sweet liquid. I am poured into a glass four times during the seder. Each of the four times reminds us of God's four promises to bring us from slavery to freedom.

   Who am I? __יַיִן__

102

Pages: 103–107
Key Word: שׁוֹפָר
New Letter: פ
Alef-Bet Flashcard: 36
Word Cards: 48, 49, 50, 51, 52

KEY WORD (שׁוֹפָר)

- What is a shofar and when is it used? [**horn sounded on Rosh Hashanah and Yom Kippur**]
- How do you feel when you hear the sound of the shofar?
- Why do we blow the shofar on Rosh Hashanah? [**reminds us that God is present; an alarm to remind us to pay attention to our lives and our actions; announcement that this day celebrates the creation of the world; reminder of when God gave us the Torah**]

INTRODUCE THE NEW LETTER – פ

Hold up *alef-bet* flashcard #34 (פ) and have the students identify the name and sound of the *pay*. Hold up *alef-bet* flashcard #36 (פ) adjacent to #34 and ask the students what is missing. [**the dot in the middle**] Then introduce the *fay* and its sound.

What other letters have almost identical forms? [ת-ת, כ-כ, ב-ב]

Direct the students to turn to page 103 and have a volunteer read the Key word at the top of the page.

READING PRACTICE
Dramatic Reading

Read the lines dramatically, as if on stage. For example, have the students read the first line as if they are the giant from Jack and the Beanstalk.

NOW READ & READ AGAIN

Call on students at random to read each of the lines. Keep students on their toes by calling on the same child more than once.

HERITAGE WORDS

נֶפֶשׁ is soul. What is a soul? **[Our souls guide us in the direction of Torah, help us to know right from wrong, and use the talents we have to the best of our ability.]** Have students think of two words that they believe describe themselves. For example: loving, talkative, musical, playful, funny etc. These are all aspects of our soul. Our souls are an important ingredient in who we are and what we do.

It is said that the sound of the שׁוֹפָר awakens our souls. What does this mean? **[The soul serves as our conscience, telling us what is the right way to behave. When we behave wrongly, it may be said that our soul is sleeping. The trumpet sound of the shofar awakens our soul so that we behave in the right and proper way.]**

What is the אֲפִיקוֹמָן? Where in the house have you found the *afikoman?*

תְּפִלָּה is the more general word used to describe the different prayers that we recite. *Brachot* are usually specific blessings recited before or after engaging in a specific action, when asking God for something, or when thanking God.

When is the הַפְטָרָה recited and what is it? **[It is recited after the Torah reading on Shabbat and holidays and consists of selections from the *nevi'im* (Prophets). There is always an aspect of the haftarah that relates to that week's Torah reading.]**

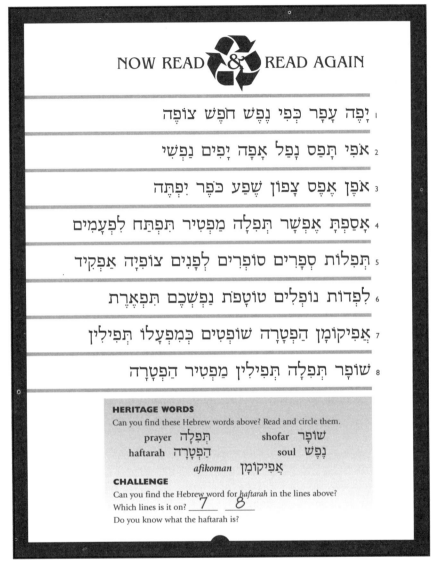

NOW READ & READ AGAIN

1 יָפֶה עָפָר כְּפִי נֶפֶשׁ חֹפֶשׁ צוֹפֶה

2 אַפִּי תָּפַס נָפַל אָפָה יָפִים נַפְשִׁי

3 אֹפֶן אֶפֶס צָפוֹן שֶׁפַע כֹּפֶר יִפְתֶּה

4 אָסַפְתָּ אֶפְשָׁר תְּפִלָּה מַפְטִיר תִּפְתַּח לִפְעָמִים

5 תְּפִלּוֹת סְפָרִים סוֹפְרִים לְפָנִים צוֹפִיָּה אַפְקִיד

6 לִפְדּוֹת נוֹפְלִים טוֹטָפֹת נַפְשְׁכֶם תִּפְאֶרֶת

7 אֲפִיקוֹמָן הַפְטָרָה שׁוֹפְטִים כְּמִפְעָלוֹ תְּפִילִין

8 שׁוֹפָר תְּפִלָּה תְּפִילִין מַפְטִיר הַפְטָרָה

HERITAGE WORDS
Can you find these Hebrew words above? Read and circle them.

prayer	תְּפִלָּה	shofar	שׁוֹפָר
haftarah	הַפְטָרָה	soul	נֶפֶשׁ
afikoman	אֲפִיקוֹמָן		

CHALLENGE
Can you find the Hebrew word for *haftarah* in the lines above?
Which lines is it on? ___7___ ___8___
Do you know what the haftarah is?

WRITE THE LETTER

Ask for a volunteer to come to the chalkboard to demonstrate how to write a *fay*. This should not be difficult since the students have already learned to write the *pay*. The rest of the class should write the *fay* in the space provided in the book.

WRITING PRACTICE

Write the Letter

פ פ פ פ

Write the Words

Write the Hebrew word for *shofar*.

שׁוֹפָר   שׁוֹפָר

Write the Hebrew word for *soul*.

נֶפֶשׁ   נֶפֶשׁ

Write the Hebrew word for *afikoman*.

אֲפִיקוֹמָן   אֲפִיקוֹמָן

Write the Hebrew word for *prayer*.

תְּפִלָּה   תְּפִלָּה

Write the Hebrew word for *haftarah*.

הַפְטָרָה   הַפְטָרָה

PRAYER BUILDING BLOCKS

Read these prayer phrases. Circle the Hebrew letters that sound the same as the English letter in the box. Write the letters you circled.

ד	תָּמִיד מְסַפְּרִים כְּבוֹד אֱלֹהִים	D 1
	אֲשֶׁר אָנֹכִי מְצַוֶּה אֶתְכֶם הַיּוֹם	M 2
	עַל לְבַבְכֶם וְעַל נַפְשְׁכֶם	V 3
	נַפְשִׁי תִדוֹם וְנַפְשִׁי כֶּעָפָר לַכֹּל תִּהְיֶה	F 4
	קְשַׁרְתֶּם אֹתָם לְאוֹת עַל יֶדְכֶם	T 5
	פּוֹתְחִים אֶת פִּיהֶם בְּשִׁירָה	P 6

105

USING THE PHOTOGRAPH

- What is the man in the photograph doing? **[sounding the shofar; teaching how to blow the shofar]**
- What do you think these children are thinking as they listen to the shofar blast?
- What is the man wearing? **[*tallit*]**

THE LIVING TRADITION

What are the names of the three notes blown on the shofar during Rosh Hashanah services and what does each sound like?

[*tekiah* – one long, clear blast
shevarim – three short mournful blasts
teruah – nine very short, staccato notes]

If possible, have someone come into class who can blow the shofar sounds and then have the students identify them.

PICTURE PERFECT

After the students complete this exercise, have them choose one of the words and write a poem or short story about that object or concept.

THE LIVING TRADITION שׁוֹפָר

The שׁוֹפָר is made from a ram's horn. When it is blown, it makes a loud trumpeting sound. We blow the שׁוֹפָר on Rosh Hashanah and Yom Kippur. In ancient times the שׁוֹפָר was blown to announce the beginning of Shabbat. The Bible tells us it was sounded at Mount Sinai when we were given God's Torah and we promised to obey God's commandments. When we hear the sound of the שׁוֹפָר today, it reminds us that we must keep that promise always.

PICTURE PERFECT

Read each word aloud.

Write the correct word below the matching picture.

טַלִּית
תּוֹרָה
שׁוֹפָר
פֶּסַח
אֲרוֹן הַקֹדֶשׁ

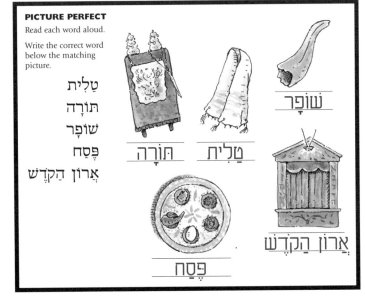

שׁוֹפָר

תּוֹרָה   טַלִּית

אֲרוֹן הַקֹדֶשׁ

פֶּסַח

CHECKPOINT

Choose from the following techniques:

1. Develop different patterns and have the students read the words in the boxes that follow the pattern. For example, read all boxes that are multiples of three – 3, 6, 9, etc.

2. Call out a box number at random and have a student name all the letters in that word.

3. Call out a Hebrew letter that has been learned and have students read all the words in the grid that contain that letter.

4. Call on students to come to the chalkboard and copy all the words in a given row.

FYI

Basic Checkpoint Technique

Use the Checkpoint to assess each student's progress. Listen to students read individually. Circle errors lightly in pencil in their textbooks. Reteach problem letters and retest students, erasing the pencil marks when they read the word correctly.

A FAMILIAR TERM

Review the meaning of *tsedakah*. Why would the phrase *keren ami* – fund of my people – be used for the money we give to *tsedakah*?

CHECKPOINT
Read the Hebrew word in each box.

דֶּלֶת 4	עֶבֶד 3	בֶּאֱמֶת 2	אֱלֹהִים 1
טֶרֶם 8	חֶסֶד 7	מִצְוָה 6	הֶבֶל 5
לֶחֶם 12	תֹּכֶן 11	כֶּתֶר 10	יִהְיֶה 9
עֶרֶב 16	סֶלַע 15	נֶאֱמָן 14	עֹמֶר 13
קֶרֶן 20	צֶדֶק 19	נֶפֶשׁ 18	פֶּסַח 17
תֶּבֶן 24	כֹּתֶל 23	אֲשֶׁר 22	פֶּרֶק 21

A FAMILIAR TERM

Do you recognize the term קֶרֶן עַמִּי? It means *"fund of my people."*

We often use this term when talking about the money we donate toward צְדָקָה.

LESSON 19

Pages: 108–113
Keyword: עֵץ חַיִּים
New Letter: ץ
New Vowels: ֵ
Alef-Bet Flashcards: 37, 38, 39
Word Cards: 53, 54, 55, 56, 57, 58

KEY WORD (עֵץ חַיִּים)

Display word card #53 (עֵץ חַיִּים). Ask the students to read the second word. What does it mean? **[life]** Point to the first letter in the first word and ask the students to name it. **[ayin]** Read the first word to the students. **[etz]** Explain that the word *etz* means "tree."

Students were introduced to the word *l'ḥayyim* in Lesson 13. What does it mean? **[to life]** What does *etz ḥayyim* mean? **[tree of life]**

- Is this phrase from the synagogue service familiar to anyone? **[part of prayer sung when returning the Torah to the Ark at the end of the Torah Service]**
- Why might it be appropriate to sing about *etz ḥayyim* at this point in the service? **[The Torah is our tree of life.]**

Sing Etz Ḥayyim Hee if your students know it.

INTRODUCING THE NEW VOWEL: ֵ

Using *alef-bet* flashcards #37 and #38, show the new vowel *tsere* to students. Compare it to the vowel *ḥirik*, which has only one dot (*alef-bet* flashcards #21 and #22). Then add the *alef-bet* flashcards for the other vowels learned, review and drill them. (5, 6, 13, 16, 21, 22, 29, 30, 32, 33)

READING PRACTICE

Read line 1 in unison and then call on students individually to read the line. Have one student read line 2 and then have the entire class repeat the line in unison. Do the same with line 3.

NOW READ & READ AGAIN

Have a child read until you clap your hands. At that time, the next student reads. Determine the number of words according to the student's ability and reading fluency, keeping the pace lively.

HERITAGE WORDS

What is a סֵדֶר? What does the word seder mean? [order] Why is this word used for the name of this important *Pesaḥ* ceremony? [There is a specific order to the evening.] What is another Hebrew word which sounds similar to seder? [siddur] A *siddur* is a book with the order of our prayers. There is a modern Hebrew phrase, בְּסֵדֶר which means OK, or more literally, everything is in order.

What is the difference between Torah and סֵפֶר תּוֹרָה? [The proper name of the object itself is *sefer Torah* – Torah scroll. "Torah" itself is the ideas and concepts contained in the scroll. We study Torah. In the synagogue, we kiss the *sefer Torah*.]

What light is always left on in the synagogue sanctuary? [נֵר תָּמִיד – eternal light] Why do all synagogues have a *ner tamid*? [It reminds us that God is always with us.]

What are other ways to say "so be it" in English? [Possible answers may include, I agree, I believe, etc.] אָמֵן literally means "I believe."

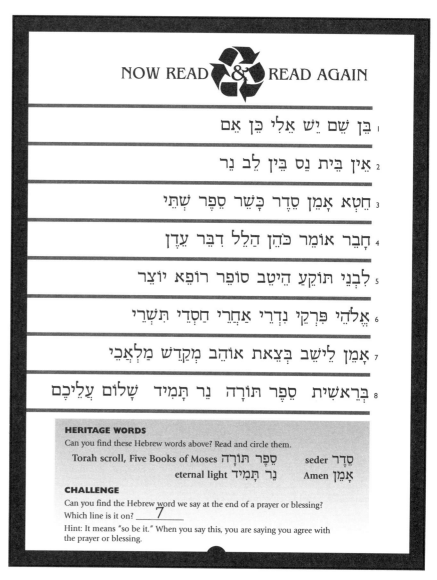

NOW READ & READ AGAIN

1 בֵּן שֵׁם יֵשׁ אֵלִי כֵּן אֵם

2 אֵין בֵּית נֵס בֵּין לֵב נֵר

3 חֵטְא אָמֵן סֵדֶר כָּשֵׁר סֵפֶר שְׁתֵי

4 חָבֵר אוֹמֵר כֹּהֵן הַלֵּל דִּבֵּר עֵדֶן

5 לִבְנֵי תּוֹקֵעַ הֵיטֵב סוֹפֵר רוֹפֵא יוֹצֵר

6 אֱלֹהֵי פִּרְקֵי נְדְרֵי אַחֲרֵי חַסְדֵי תִּשְׁרֵי

7 אָמֵן לֵישֵׁב בְּצֵאת אוֹהֵב מִקְדַּשׁ מַלְאֲכֵי

8 בְּרֵאשִׁית סֵפֶר תּוֹרָה נֵר תָּמִיד שָׁלוֹם עֲלֵיכֶם

HERITAGE WORDS

Can you find these Hebrew words above? Read and circle them.

Torah scroll, Five Books of Moses סֵפֶר תּוֹרָה   seder סֵדֶר

eternal light נֵר תָּמִיד   Amen אָמֵן

CHALLENGE

Can you find the Hebrew word we say at the end of a prayer or blessing?
Which line is it on? _____7_____

Hint: It means "so be it." When you say this, you are saying you agree with the prayer or blessing.

RHYME TIME

Ask the students to read aloud the two rhyming words on each line. Challenge the class to find other rhyming words in the eight lines of the exercise. For example, קוֹרֵא – line 3, first word; פִּרְקֵי – line 8, fourth word.

INTRODUCE THE NEW LETTER – ץ

Write the phrase *etz ḥayyim* on the chalkboard. Call on a student to read the first word aloud. What does it mean? **[tree]** Point to the final *tsadee* in the word and ask which letter looks similar to this. **[tsadee]** How do the two letters differ? **[final tsadee has a tail]** Hold *alef-bet* flashcards #20 and #39 next to each other. Explain that *alef-bet* flashcard #39 is a *final tsadee*. What two other Hebrew letters learned so far also have a final form? **[Nun and mem]**

Have the class read the entire phrase written on the chalkboard in unison and then call on individuals to read it.

READING PRACTICE

Divide the class into three groups and have each group read one of the three lines in unison. Alternate until each group has read each line.

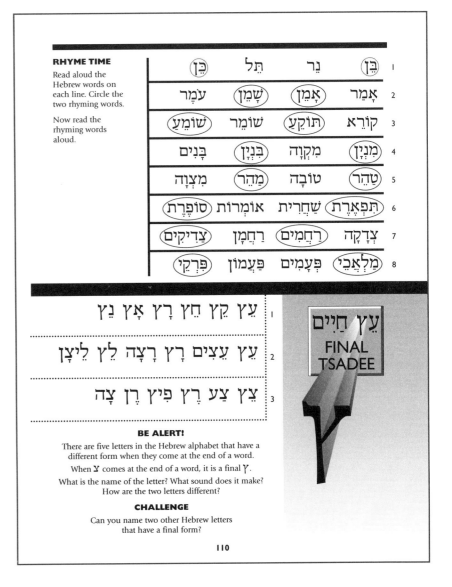

RHYME TIME

Read aloud the Hebrew words on each line. Circle the two rhyming words.

Now read the rhyming words aloud.

בֵּן	תֵּל	נֵר	בֵּן	1
עֹמֶר	שֶׁמֶן	אָמֵן	אָמַר	2
שׁוֹמֵעַ	שׁוֹמֵר	תּוֹקֵעַ	קוֹרֵא	3
בָּנִים	בִּנְיָן	מִקְוֶה	מִנְיָן	4
מִצְוָה	מַהֵר	טוֹבָה	טָהֵר	5
סוֹפֶרֶת	אוֹמְרוֹת	שַׁחֲרִית	תִּפְאֶרֶת	6
צַדִּיקִים	רַחֲמָן	רַחֲמִים	צְדָקָה	7
פִּרְקֵי	פַּעֲמוֹן	פְּעָמִים	מַלְאֲכֵי	8

עֵץ חַיִּים
FINAL TSADEE

עֵץ קֵץ חֵץ רָץ אָץ נֵץ 1

עֵץ עֵצִים רָץ רָצָה לֵץ לֵיצָן 2

צֵץ צַע רֶץ פִּיץ רֶן צָה 3

BE ALERT!

There are five letters in the Hebrew alphabet that have a different form when they come at the end of a word.

When צ comes at the end of a word, it is a final ץ.

What is the name of the letter? What sound does it make? How are the two letters different?

CHALLENGE

Can you name two other Hebrew letters that have a final form?

110

NOW READ & READ AGAIN

Call on a student to read the first three words on line 1. Then call on another student to read the next three words until all the words have been read.

When recycling this exercise, ask the students to follow these instructions for each line:

Line #	Instructions
1)	Read the words that contain a *mem*
2)	Read the words that begin with a *kuf*
3)	Read the words that contain a *tsadee*
4)	Read the words that contain a *tsere*
5)	Read the words that contain a final *tsadee*
6)	Read the words that contain a *segol*
7)	Read the words that contain a *hirik*
8)	Read the four words that conclude the blessing we recite before eating bread

HERITAGE WORDS

After the students complete the challenge exercise, ask them why we eat matzah and not חָמֵץ on *Pesah*. [**The Israelites' bread dough did not have time to rise when they left Egypt.**]

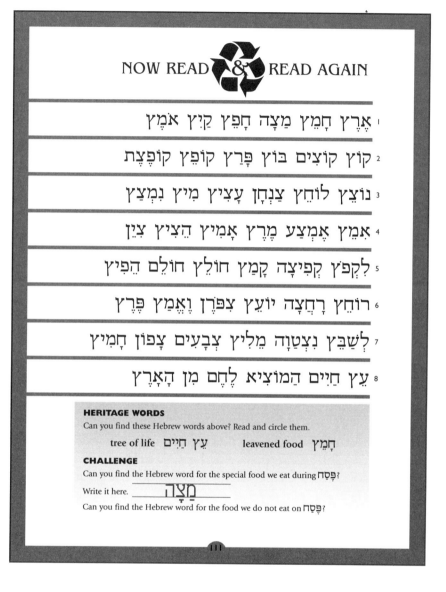

WRITE THE LETTER

Have the students complete the writing practice exercises as in previous lessons. Ensure that the students are forming the *final tsadee* correctly and are writing part of the letter outside of the ruled lines.

BE ALERT

Here are the meanings of the 12 Hebrew words in the "Be Alert" exercise.

1) tree
2) the land
3) crayons, colors
4) brings forth; part of blessing recited over bread
5) unleavened bread
6) leavened food
7) commanded
8) name of vowel (*kamatz*): ָ
9) commandment
10) justice; *tsedakah*
11) jump
12) a just or righteous person

Which two pairs of the 12 Hebrew words listed are related?

[מִצְוָה-צִוָה ,צְדָקָה-צַדִיק]

WRITING PRACTICE

Write the Letter

ץ ץ ץ

Write the Words

Write the Hebrew words for *tree of life.*

עֵץ חַיִּים

Write the Hebrew word for *leavened food.*

חָמֵץ

Write the Hebrew words for *Torah scroll.*

סֵפֶר תּוֹרָה

Write the Hebrew words for *Eternal Light.*

נֵר תָּמִיד

Write the Hebrew word for *seder.*

סֵדֶר

Write the Hebrew word for *amen.*

אָמֵן

BE ALERT!

The letters צ and ץ make the same sound. How are they different? Complete each word by adding the correct form of the *tsadee*. How many words can you read?

9 מִצְוָה	5 מַצָּה	1 עֵץ
10 צְדָקָה	6 חָמֵץ	2 הָאָרֶץ
11 קוֹפֵץ	7 צִוָה	3 צִבְעִים
12 צַדִיק	8 קָמָץ	4 הַמוֹצִיא

Do you know the meaning of some of the words? How many? _____

112

UNDERSTANDING THE PHOTOGRAPH

- What is the man in the picture doing? **[lifting a *sefer Torah*]**
- What is he holding on to? **[the Torah's *atzei ḥayyim* – plural of *etz ḥayyim*]**
- When would this usually be done? **[during synagogue services, after the Torah reading]**

THE LIVING TRADITION

Bring a *sefer Torah* to the classroom or arrange for the class to visit the synagogue's sanctuary to look at one close up. Allow the students to touch the wooden staves of the *sefer Torah*. How do they feel when they touch them? Explain that these are actually called *atzei ḥayyim*—trees of life. Ask the students why they think that the staves are known by this name. **[There is no definitive answer. In addition to the explanantion given in the textbook, one might also say that the staves are the roots and trunk of the Torah which hold up its branches and leaves—the parchment which contains God's words.]**

Open up the Torah and show the students that there are no vowels in the Torah. Using a *yad* (Torah pointer), point out a word or two that the students already know. Prepare in advance so that you will know that there are appropriate words in the section to which the scroll is rolled. Ask if any of the students can read the words as you point to them.

CONNECTIONS

Ask the students if they can translate any of the phrases they completed in this exercise. Some of these words have not yet been taught.

1. *ḥamotzi leḥem* – who brings forth bread
2. *mah nisḥtanah* – how is [this night] different
3. *etz ḥayyim* – tree of life
4. *sefer Torah* – Torah scroll
5. *y'tziat mitzrayim* – the Exodus (going out) from Egypt
6. *yom tov* – literally means "good day"; holiday
7. *aron hakodesh* – the holy ark
8. *ner tamid* – eternal light

THE LIVING TRADITION עֵץ חַיִּים

A tree of life—עֵץ חַיִּים—is one of the symbols of the תּוֹרָה. In fact, the two wooden rollers around which the תּוֹרָה scroll is wrapped are called עֲצֵי חַיִּים—trees of life. The תּוֹרָה is like a tree because just as a tree is strong and offers food, so too the Torah gives the Jewish people strength and nourishes our souls.

CONNECTIONS

Connect the beginning of a phrase with its ending. Read the complete phrases with a partner.

AN *ALEF BET* CHART

You have learned five new letters in Lessons 15-19:

ט פ ס פ ץ.

Turn to the *Alef Bet* Chart on page 160. Color in the new letters.
How many letters do you know?
Can you say the name and sound of each letter?

113

---

9. *shana tovah* – literally means "good year;" traditional Rosh Hashanah greeting
10. *shalom aleichem* – peace be with you

LESSON 20

Pages: 114–118
Key Word: יִשְׂרָאֵל
New Letter: שׂ
Alef-Bet Flashcard: 40
Word Cards: 59, 60, 61

REVIEW EXERCISE

I Spy

Say, "I spy a *lamed*" or "I spy an '*ah*' sound." Call on a student to come up to the *alef-bet* chart and point to the correct letter or vowel. Next, it is the student's turn to "spy" a letter or vowel. Then have that student call on a classmate to come up and find it.

KEY WORD (יִשְׂרָאֵל)

Display a map of Israel. Ask if anyone knows what country it is. Have any of the students been to Israel? If so, have them share their impressions of the experience.

Why is Israel so important to the Jewish people? **[the Jewish state, birthplace of the Jewish People, etc.]** What do they think it would be like to live in Israel?

INTRODUCE THE NEW LETTER – שׂ

Announce "I spy a *sin*!" and point to the *sin* on the *alef-bet* chart. Hold up word card #59 (יִשְׂרָאֵל), read the word, and point to the *sin*. What sound does the *sin* make? What letter does the *sin* look like? **[shin]** How is it different from the *shin*? **[location of the dot]** What other letter has an "s" sound? **[samech]**

READING PRACTICE

Randomly call on students to read each of these three lines

NOW READ & READ AGAIN

Have one student read a line and then have that student call out the name of the next reader.

For further reading practice, continue the "I spy" theme by announcing sounds at random from the three lines. For example, "I spy the third word on the second line." Then the student who is called on to read that sound should "spy" a new sound and select a classmate to recite it.

HERITAGE WORDS

עֲשֶׂרֶת הַדִּבְּרוֹת literally means "the ten sayings" or "the ten utterances." Why were the Ten Commandments given this name? [**the words were said or uttered by God**] What is the Hebrew word for commandments? [מִצְוֹת]

Can you list each of the Ten Commandments?
1. God is One and there is no other
2. You shall worship no other Gods
3. You shall not speak falsely in God's name
4. Remember the Sabbath day, to keep it holy
5. Honor your father and your mother
6. You shall not murder
7. You shall not be false to your wife or husband
8. You shall not steal
9. You shall not lie
10. You shall not want things that belong to someone else

Have you ever heard someone say that something is a *simḥah*? This means that it is a happy event and comes from the word שָׂמֵחַ, which means "happy."

WORD RIDDLE

Answer: שִׂמְחַת תּוֹרָה

NOW READ & READ AGAIN

1. שֶׂה שִׂים שַׂר שָׂם שַׂק שִׂיא

2. שָׂרָה שָׂנֵא שָׂמַח עֶשֶׂר עֹשֶׂה מַשָׂא

3. שָׂרָה שָׂרָה שָׂמָה שָׂמָה שַׂעַר שָׂשׂוֹן

4. שֵׂעָר שָׂכָר שָׂפָה יִשָׂא בָּשָׂר שֵׂכֶל

5. שָׂדֶה פָּשַׂט שֶׂבַע עֶשֶׂר עָשָׂה תַּיִשׁ

6. שִׂמְחַת תּוֹרָה שְׁמוֹנֶה עֲשָׂרָה עֲשֶׂרֶת הַדִּבְּרוֹת

7. שְׁמַע יִשְׂרָאֵל שִׂים שָׂלוֹם עוֹשֶׂה שָׂלוֹם

8. עַם יִשְׂרָאֵל בְּנֵי יִשְׂרָאֵל אֶרֶץ יִשְׂרָאֵל

HERITAGE WORDS

Can you find these Hebrew words above? Read and circle them.

Ten Commandments עֲשֶׂרֶת הַדִּבְּרוֹת   Israel יִשְׂרָאֵל
Rejoicing of the Torah שִׂמְחַת תּוֹרָה

WORD RIDDLE

I am a holiday we celebrate each year when we finish reading the entire תּוֹרָה.
We then begin reading the תּוֹרָה from the very first word all over again.

My name begins with a שׂ. What holiday am I?

115

PRAYER BUILDING BLOCKS

Have students work together in pairs and correct each other as they take turns reading complete lines.

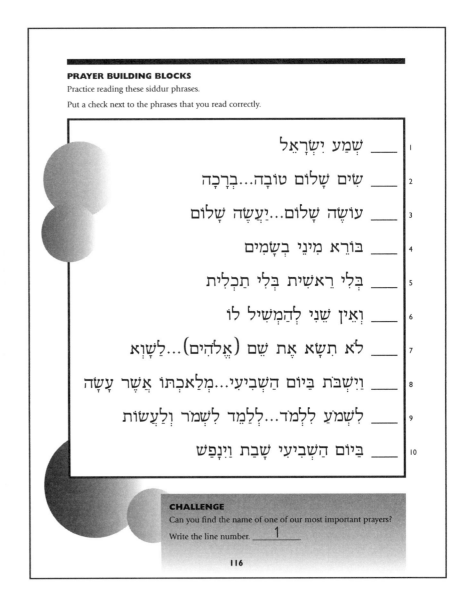

PRAYER BUILDING BLOCKS

Practice reading these siddur phrases.

Put a check next to the phrases that you read correctly.

____ שְׁמַע יִשְׂרָאֵל   1

____ שִׂים שָׁלוֹם טוֹבָה...בְּרָכָה   2

____ עוֹשֶׂה שָׁלוֹם...יַעֲשֶׂה שָׁלוֹם   3

____ בּוֹרֵא מִינֵי בְשָׂמִים   4

____ בְּלִי רֵאשִׁית בְּלִי תַכְלִית   5

____ וְאֵין שֵׁנִי לְהַמְשִׁיל לוֹ   6

____ לֹא תִשָּׂא אֶת שֵׁם (אֱלֹהִים)...לַשָּׁוְא   7

____ וַיִּשְׁבֹּת בַּיּוֹם הַשְּׁבִיעִי...מְלַאכְתּוֹ אֲשֶׁר עָשָׂה   8

____ לִשְׁמֹעַ לִלְמֹד...לְלַמֵּד לִשְׁמֹר וְלַעֲשׂוֹת   9

____ בַּיּוֹם הַשְּׁבִיעִי שָׁבַת וַיִּנָּפַשׁ   10

CHALLENGE

Can you find the name of one of our most important prayers?

Write the line number. _____1_____

116

WRITING PRACTICE

It has been a few lessons since we reminded you that *Shalom Uvrachah* [the student's edition] is available in two versions—one for teaching print writing and one for teaching script. This universal Teacher's Edition can be used with either version. You can see samples of every letter in script format on page xiv.

WRITE THE LETTER

Ask for a volunteer to come to the chalkboard to demonstrate how to write a *sin*. This should not be difficult since the students have already learned to write the *shin*.

SOUNDS LIKE

Have students complete this exercise independently. Then call on students to read a line aloud, identify the two identical Hebrew sounds, and write these two sounds on the chalkboard.

WRITING PRACTICE

Write the Letter

שׂ שׂ שׂ שׂ

Write the Words

Write the Hebrew word for *Israel*.

יִשְׂרָאֵל יִשְׂרָאֵל

Write the Hebrew words for *Rejoicing of the Torah*.

שִׂמְחַת תּוֹרָה שִׂמְחַת תּוֹרָה

SOUNDS LIKE

Read each line aloud.

Circle the Hebrew sounds on each line that are the same.

Write the sounds you circled.

עַד אַד

עַד אַד	צַד	אַד	אֵם	עַד	1
	סַם	בַּס	שָׁם	כַּס	2
	צַל	לוֹ	עוֹל	לֹא	3
	כְּכָל	כָּל	קוֹל	יָכוֹל	4
	תֵּוֶת	בִּיתָה	טַבַּת	תָּוֶת	5
	אָשֵׁר	אָסָה	עֹשֶׂר	עוֹשֶׂה	6
	בּוֹכֶה	בּוֹקֶר	קָפֵר	כּוֹפֵר	7
	עָרְסוֹת	עָשִׂיתִי	אָסִיתִי	עֲשָׂרוֹת	8

BE ALERT!
The letters שׂ and ס make the same sound.
What sound do they make?

117

USING THE PHOTOGRAPH

Where was this photograph taken? **[Israel, Jerusalem]**
How do you know? **[Israeli flags, Western Wall]**

THE LIVING TRADITION

Ask someone who has visited Israel to come to speak to the class about what it is like there. If possible, try to ask a teenager who went to Israel as part of a summer program. Make sure they bring photos or videos to show the major sights.

Try to obtain Israeli product labels that have logos the students will be familiar with. For example: Coca-Cola, Ben and Jerry's Ice Cream, etc. Also try to display Israeli children's books, comics, newspapers, etc.

TOURING יִשְׂרָאֵל

1. Safed
2. Tel Aviv
3. Eilat
4. Herzliya
5. Masada
6. Haifa
7. Jerusalem
8. Beersheba

THE LIVING TRADITION יִשְׂרָאֵל

Jewish people have lived in יִשְׂרָאֵל for more than 3,000 years. It is the country where our ancestors Abraham and Sarah lived. It is the country where King David ruled. יִשְׂרָאֵל is the country where the modern state of Israel, our homeland, was reborn. יִשְׂרָאֵל has a special place in the hearts of Jews around the world.

THINK ABOUT IT

Have you or anyone you know visited יִשְׂרָאֵל?

Which cities and places did they visit?

TOURING יִשְׂרָאֵל

Below are the names of eight places in יִשְׂרָאֵל.

Read the Hebrew name of each place aloud.

Then look at the map of יִשְׂרָאֵל.

These eight places are labeled on the map with their English names. Write the matching number next to each English name.

1 צְפַת
2 תֵּל־אָבִיב
3 אֵילַת
4 הֶרְצְלִיָה
5 מְצָדָה
6 חֵיפָה
7 יְרוּשָׁלַיִם
8 בְּאֵר שֶׁבַע

Haifa •   • Safed

Herzliya •
Tel Aviv •

  • Jerusalem

Masada •

Beersheba •

Eilat •

118

LESSON 21

Pages: 119–126
Key Word: חַג שָׂמֵחַ
New Letter: ג
Alef-Bet Flashcard: 41
Word Cards: 62, 63, 64, 65, 66

KEY WORD (חַג שָׂמֵחַ)

Display word card #62 (חַג שָׂמֵחַ) and have the students read the second
word. What does *sameah* mean? **[happy]** Read the entire phrase and
define it. **[traditional holiday greeting – "happy holiday"]** Have the
students list occasions when you might wish someone a *hag sameah*.
[Simhat Torah, Sukkot, *Pesah*, etc.] Have the students practice saying
hag sameah to one another.

INTRODUCE THE NEW LETTER – ג

Print the word סְבִיבוֹן on the chalkboard and ask the students to read
and identify the word. **[dreidel]** What letters are on a *s'vivon*? **[ש נ ג ה]**
Although the students have not formally learned the *gimmel* yet, they
may be familiar with it from the dreidel game. Point to the *gimmel* on the
alef-bet chart and on word card #62. Formally teach the *gimmel* to the
class. Next point to the *nun* on the *alef-bet* chart. How do the *gimmel*
and *nun* differ in appearance?

READING PRACTICE

Continuing with the *s'vivon* theme, write on the chalkboard the rules for
the *Shalom Uvrachah* version of the dreidel game.

  Gimmel – read no lines
    Nun – read line 1
    Hay – read lines 1 and 2
    Shin – read lines 1, 2, and 3

Each student, in turn, spins a dreidel and then follows the rules above.

NOW READ & READ AGAIN

Record each student as they read one of the lines. Two or three weeks later have the students, in the same order, read the same line on a second tape. Play back both and compare. This method allows the students to hear proof of their improvement.

HERITAGE WORDS

Magen means "shield" but because the symbol is star shaped many people translate the phrase מָגֵן דָּוִד as "star of David" or "Jewish star." Some people say that King David had a shield shaped like a *magen David*. How many points are there on a *magen David*? **[6]**

Why is the book we use at the *Pesaḥ* seder called a הַגָּדָה? (meaning "telling") **[The *haggadah* contains the story of the Israelites' Exodus from Egypt to freedom.]**

Explain to the students that a מְגִלָּה is a scroll in which the parchment is rolled up and tied closed or is wound around one stave or roller. An example is *megilat Esther*, which is read on Purim. How does this scroll differ from a Torah scroll? **[With a Torah scroll, the parchment is connected to two staves or rollers.]**

NOW READ & READ AGAIN

1 חַג גַּן גְּדִי גֵּר דָּג גַּם

2 גֹּלֶם גָּדַל מָגֵן עֹנֶג גֶּפֶן גִּיל

3 גִּבּוֹר גּוֹלֵל גּוֹמֵל גָּאַל גֶּשֶׁם דֶּגֶל

4 גּוֹלָה מְגִלָּה הִשִּׂיג מִנְהָג גָּדוֹל גִּטִּים

5 אַגָּדָה אֶתְרֹג רֶגֶל הִגְדִּיל חַגִּים גְּדוֹלָה

6 גְּמָרָא נְגִילָה הִגִּיעַ חֲגִיגָה שִׁגָּעוֹן פִּתְגָם

7 מָגֵן אַבְרָהָם מְגִלָּה עֹנֶג שַׁבָּת יִתְגַּדַּל

8 הַגָּדָה חַד גַּדְיָא מָגֵן דָּוִד מָגֵן אָבוֹת

HERITAGE WORDS

Can you find these Hebrew words above? Read and circle them.

scroll מְגִלָּה   *haggadah* הַגָּדָה

Shield of David, Jewish star מָגֵן דָּוִד

CHALLENGE

The Jewish star is known as the *Magen David*—the Shield of David. This symbol is found on the flag of Israel. Can you find the Hebrew words for *Magen David*? Which line are they on? ___8___

120

SEARCH AND CIRCLE

Have the students complete the exercise independently. Before reviewing as a group, write the following Hebrew letters on the chalkboard and ask the students to circle the line number in which the boxed English sound matches the Hebrew sound – צ ב ס נ מ ת. Then ask the students to name the other Hebrew letter that has that sound.

2. *Tav*
3. *Mem*
4. *Nun*
5. *Samech*
6. *Vet*
9. *Tsadee*

READING PRACTICE

Have the students look at the key word and point to the *ḥet* at the end of *sameaḥ*. Explain the special rule that applies in these cases, as noted in the Be Alert section. Call on students to read the entire phrase.

Have students randomly read words from these three lines. Emphasize the "ḥ" sound.

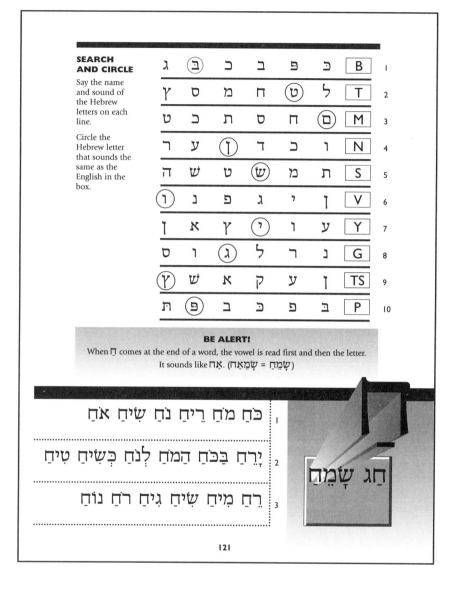

NOW READ & READ AGAIN

Call on students to read a line of text aloud. For a change of pace, first read all the odd-numbered lines followed by the even-numbered lines.

HERITAGE WORDS

What do we believe will happen when the מָשִׁיחַ comes? **[There will be peace in the world.]** According to our tradition who will anounce that the messiah is about to come? **[Elijah the Prophet]** When do we sing the song *Eliyahu Hanavi*, about our hope that Elijah will come soon to announce the coming of the messiah? **[Havdalah at the end of Shabbat; during the Pesaḥ seder.]**

NOW READ & READ AGAIN

1. שָׂמֵחַ יָרֵחַ אוֹרֵחַ נָשִׁיחַ מֵנִיחַ בַּכֹּחַ

2. מָשִׁיחַ פּוֹקֵחַ סוֹלֵחַ פּוֹתֵחַ פָּתַח לִפְתֹּחַ

3. לְשַׁבֵּחַ מְנַצֵּחַ שׁוֹלֵחַ מָנוֹחַ שָׁלִיחַ מַפְתֵּחַ

4. מַצְמִיחַ מִשְׁלוֹחַ הִצְלִיחַ לוֹקֵחַ לִשְׂמֵחַ פּוֹרֵחַ

5. מַשְׁגִּיחַ הַשְׁגָּחָה אָשִׁיחַ שִׂיחָה מְשַׂמֵּחַ שָׂמַח

6. הִבְטִיחַ בָּטַח טוֹרֵחַ טָרַח פְּקֵחַ נִפְקַח

7. בּוֹרֵחַ לִבְרֹחַ בָּרַח לִסְלֹחַ סָלַח סְלִיחָה

8. מָשִׁיחַ חַג שָׂמֵחַ פֶּסַח הַגָּדָה מְגִלָּה

HERITAGE WORDS
Can you find these Hebrew words above? Read and circle them.

Messiah מָשִׁיחַ   happy holiday חַג שָׂמֵחַ

CHALLENGE
How many times did you read the word for *Messiah*? ___2___

PRAYER TIME

The following are translations of each of the prayer phrases, as well as the occasions when that blessing is recited.

1. creator of fruit of the vine (e.g., over grapes, wine)
2. creator of fruit of the tree (e.g., over apples, oranges)
3. creator of fruit of the ground (e.g., over potatoes, carrots)
4. creator of the lights of fire (recited during *Havdalah*)
5. creator of different spices (recited during *Havdalah*)

Which word is identical in each of these prayer endings? [**בּוֹרֵא**] What do you think it means? [**creator**]

PRAYER BUILDING BLOCKS

Practice reading these siddur phrases.

Put a check next to the phrases that you read correctly.

1. ____ לְשַׁבֵּחַ לַאֲדוֹן הַכֹּל

2. ____ הָאֵל הַגָּדוֹל הַגִּבּוֹר וְהַנּוֹרָא

3. ____ לְעֵת תָּכִין מַטְבֵּחַ

4. ____ לְהוֹדוֹת לְהַלֵּל לְשַׁבֵּחַ

5. ____ שְׂמֵחִים בְּצֵאתָם וְשָׂשִׂים בְּבֹאָם

6. ____ מְשַׂמֵּחַ צִיּוֹן בְּבָנֶיהָ

PRAYER TIME

Practice reading these endings to familiar בְּרָכוֹת.

Do you know when we recite each one?

1. בּוֹרֵא פְּרִי הַגָּפֶן

2. בּוֹרֵא פְּרִי הָעֵץ

3. בּוֹרֵא פְּרִי הָאֲדָמָה

4. בּוֹרֵא מְאוֹרֵי הָאֵשׁ

5. בּוֹרֵא מִינֵי בְשָׂמִים

THE ADDED DOT

Add a dot to one member of each set of family letters.

Write the sound of each letter on the line below the letter.

ת ת	פ פ	כ כ	ב ב
T T	F P	CH K	V B

Which letter did not change its sound when you added a dot? ת ת

123

RHYME TIME

Read the instructions and have the students complete the exercise independently.

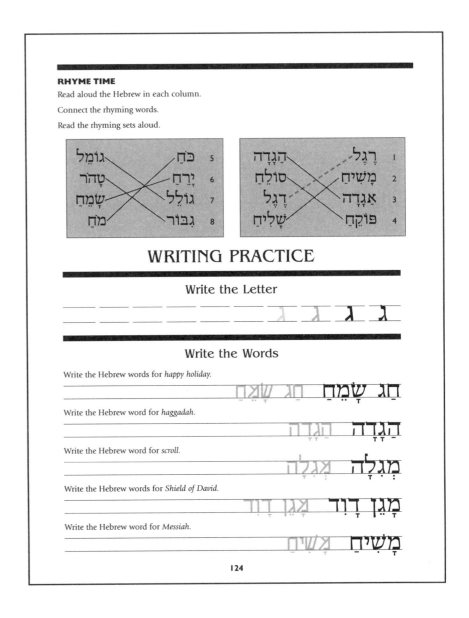

USING THE PHOTOGRAPH

- What holiday are the children celebrating? **[Purim]**
- How do you know? **[children wearing costumes, twirling *graggers*]**
- How should these students greet each other? **[*ḥag sameaḥ*]**

THE LIVING TRADITION

What are things that we can do on each holiday to help make it a *ḥag sameaḥ*?

WORD WIZARD

1. What special holiday greeting do we use on Rosh Hashanah? **[*shanah tovah*]**

2. Why do you think that we wish each other "a peaceful Shabbat" instead of "a happy Shabbat"? **[While Shabbat is a happy and joyous day, the overall theme of the day is that we rest on Shabbat. Therefore, we want Shabbat to be a peaceful and restful day.]**

THE LIVING TRADITION חַג שָׂמֵחַ

The word חַג means "holiday" or "festival." The word שָׂמֵחַ means "happy" or "joyous." When we say חַג שָׂמֵחַ, we wish someone a *happy holiday*.

WORD WIZARD

Discover a hidden word.

Cross out the Hebrew letters and their vowels that match the English sounds.

Write the remaining Hebrew letters and their vowels to discover a hidden word.

1.

1 SAY	4 M	7 SHOH
2 TEH	5 PEH	8 GEH
3 NEE	6 VEE	9 HAH

פְּשָׂיִמֶשׁוּגֶחַ   סִיחַטֶנִיגֵם

חַ   מֶ   שׂ   ג   ח

What does it mean? ___Happy Holiday___

When do we use it? ___Holiday greeting___

2.

1 YAH	4 SAH	7 KAH
2 FOH	5 N	8 EH
3 CHAH	6 GEE	9 DAY
		10 TS

גִיקְשָׂצֶלוּדָיםֶ   זְפוּשָׁאַבַשֶׁתַץ

ם   לֹ   שׁ   תַ   בַּ   שׁ

What does it mean? ___a peaceful Shabbat___

When do we use it? ___Shabbat greeting___

125

CHECKPOINT

Choose from the following techniques:

1. Develop different patterns and have the students read the words in the boxes that follow the pattern. For example, read all boxes that are multiples of four – 4, 8, 12, etc.

2. Call out a box number at random and have a student name all the letters in that word.

3. Call out a vowel that has been learned and have students read all the words in the grid which contain that vowel.

4. Call on students to come to the chalkboard and write all the words that are only one syllable. **[1, 8, 11, 23]**

FYI

Basic Checkpoint Technique

Use the Checkpoint to assess each student's progress. Listen to students read individually. Circle errors lightly in pencil in their textbooks. Reteach problem letters and retest students, erasing the pencil marks when they read the word correctly.

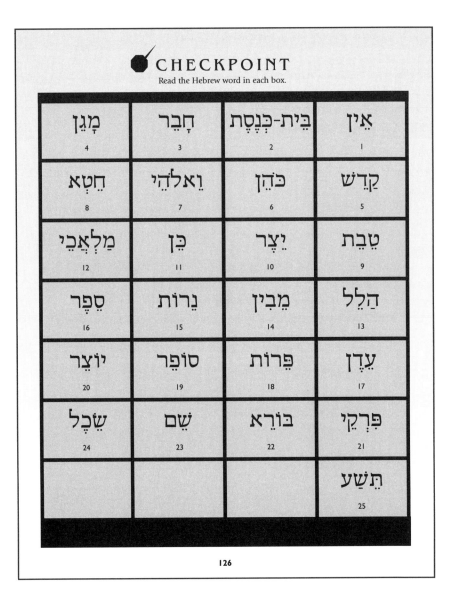

CHECKPOINT
Read the Hebrew word in each box.

מָגֵן 4	חָבֵר 3	בֵּית־כְּנֶסֶת 2	אֵין 1
חֵטְא 8	וֵאלֹהֵי 7	כֹּהֵן 6	קַדֵשׁ 5
מַלְאֲכֵי 12	כֵּן 11	יֵצֶר 10	טֵבֵת 9
סֵפֶר 16	נֵרוֹת 15	מֵבִין 14	הַלֵל 13
יוֹצֵר 20	סוֹפֵר 19	פֵּרוֹת 18	עֵדֶן 17
שֵׂכֶל 24	שֵׁם 23	בּוֹרֵא 22	פִּרְקֵי 21
			תֵּשַׁע 25

126

LESSON 22

Pages: 127–131
Key Word: קִדוּשׁ
New Vowels: וּ
Alef-Bet Flashcards: 42, 43
Word Cards: 67, 68, 69, 70, 71, 72

KEY WORD (קִדוּשׁ)

On Shabbat and on a *ḥag* we fulfill the mitzvah of declaring the day holy by reciting which prayer over wine or grape juice? **[Kiddush]**

What does it mean to be holy? **[being special, different, unique, etc.]**

Have the students complete the following sentence: "I feel holy when _____."

INTRODUCE NEW VOWELS – (SHURUK: וּ and KUBUTZ: ◌ֻ)

Display *alef-bet* flashcard #42 (וּ) and introduce its sound to the students. Then display *alef-bet* flashcards #18 (וֹ) and #29 (וֹ). Have the students identify these two cards and describe how they differ from the *shuruk*.

Hold up *alef-bet* flashcard #43 (◌ֻ) next to *alef-bet* flash card #42 (וּ) and explain that both have the same sound. What other vowels are similar in appearance to the *kubutz* and in what way do they differ? **[segol, shvah, tsere, ḥirik – number and/or configuration of dots]**

Display word cards #19 (קַדִישׁ – Kaddish), #35 (קָדוֹשׁ – holy), and #67 (קִדוּשׁ – Kiddush). Have the students read and define each of these words. What is similar to each of these words? **[קדשׁ – the root letters meaning "holy"]**

READING PRACTICE

Randomly call on individuals to read each of the three lines.

NOW READ & READ AGAIN

Call on students at random to read lines 1–8.

HERITAGE WORDS

Another name for the Torah is חֻמָשׁ. The word *ḥumash* comes from the word *ḥamesh* (five) and refers to the fact that the Torah comprises five books. What are the five books of the Torah?
[Genesis – *Bereshit*, Exodus – *Shemot*, Leviticus –*Vayikra*, Numbers – *Be'midbar*, Deuteronomy – *Devarim*]

What is the capital of Israel? [יְרוּשָׁלַיִם]

Who is supposed to announce that the Messiah will be coming?
[אֵלִיָּהוּ הַנָּבִיא]

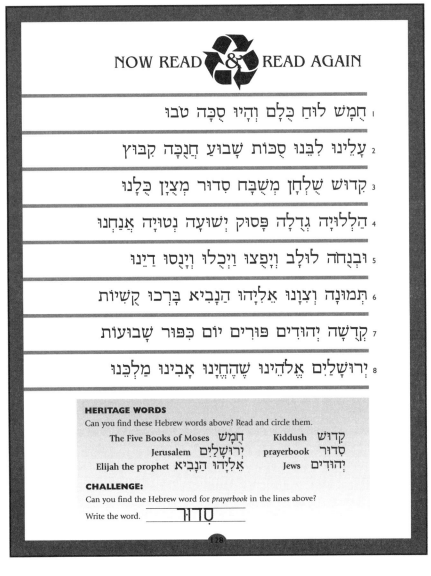

NOW READ & READ AGAIN

1. חֻמָשׁ לוּחַ כֻּלָּם וְהָיוּ סֻכָּה טָבוּ

2. עָלֵינוּ לְבְנוּ סֻכּוֹת שָׁבוּעַ חֲנֻכָּה קִבּוּץ

3. קָדוֹשׁ שֻׁלְחָן מְשֻׁבָּח סִדּוּר מְצֻיָּן כֻּלָּנוּ

4. הַלְלוּיָהּ גְּדֻלָּה פָּסוּק יְשׁוּעָה נְטוּיָה אֲנַחְנוּ

5. וּבְנָחֹה לוּלָב וְיָפְצוּ וַיִּכְלוּ וְיָנֻסוּ דַּיֵּנוּ

6. תְּמוּנָה וְצִוָּנוּ אֵלִיָּהוּ הַנָּבִיא בָּרְכוּ קָשׁוֹת

7. קָדְשָׁה יְהוּדִים פּוּרִים יוֹם כִּפּוּר שָׁבוּעוֹת

8. יְרוּשָׁלַיִם אֱלֹהֵינוּ שֶׁהֶחֱיָנוּ אָבִינוּ מַלְכֵּנוּ

HERITAGE WORDS

Can you find these Hebrew words above? Read and circle them.

The Five Books of Moses	חֻמָשׁ	Kiddush	קִדּוּשׁ
Jerusalem	יְרוּשָׁלַיִם	prayerbook	סִדּוּר
Elijah the prophet	אֵלִיָּהוּ הַנָּבִיא	Jews	יְהוּדִים

CHALLENGE:

Can you find the Hebrew word for *prayerbook* in the lines above?

Write the word. ___סִדּוּר___

128

POWER READING

Call on students to read each of these six phrases from the Shabbat Evening Kiddush. Afterwards, the teacher should sing or read aloud the full text of the Kiddush. As each phrase in the textbook is recited, the students should raise their hands. Pause, compliment the students, tell them to lower their hands, and then continue. Repeat this procedure until the end of the Kiddush.

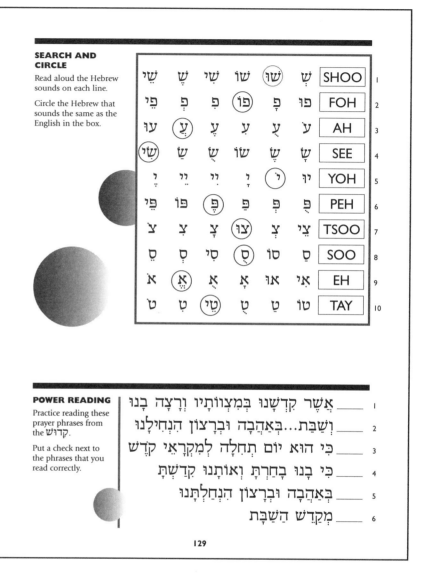

SEARCH AND CIRCLE

Read aloud the Hebrew sounds on each line.

Circle the Hebrew that sounds the same as the English in the box.

שֻׁי	שֻׁ	שִׁי	שׁוּ	שׁוּ	שׁ	SHOO	1
פֵּי	פֵּ	פָ	פּוּ	פָּ	פוּ	FOH	2
עוּ	עֲ	עַ	עֶ	עָ	עַ	AH	3
שִׁי	שֵׁ	שֶׁ	שׁוּ	שֶׁ	שָׁ	SEE	4
יְ	יִ	יֵי	יָ	יוֹ	יוּ	YOH	5
פֵּי	פּוֹ	פֵּ	פֵּ	פֵּ	פֵּ	PEH	6
צָ	צָ	צָ	צוּ	צָ	צִי	TSOO	7
סֶ	סֶ	סִי	סֻ	סוֹ	סַ	SOO	8
א	אֶ	אָ	אָ	אוּ	אִי	EH	9
ט	טִ	טִי	טֶ	טַ	טוֹ	TAY	10

POWER READING

Practice reading these prayer phrases from the קִדוּשׁ.

Put a check next to the phrases that you read correctly.

_____ אֲשֶׁר קִדְּשָׁנוּ בְּמִצְווֹתָיו וְרָצָה בָנוּ ₁

_____ וְשַׁבָּת...בְּאַהֲבָה וּבְרָצוֹן הִנְחִילָנוּ ₂

_____ כִּי הוּא יוֹם תְּחִלָּה לְמִקְרָאֵי קֹדֶשׁ ₃

_____ כִּי בָנוּ בָחַרְתָּ וְאוֹתָנוּ קִדַּשְׁתָּ ₄

_____ בְּאַהֲבָה וּבְרָצוֹן הִנְחַלְתָּנוּ ₅

_____ מְקַדֵּשׁ הַשַׁבָּת ₆

129

CHALLENGE

Many words in our prayers end with the suffix נוּ because our prayers are not just for us as individuals, but also for the benefit of the entire community.

PRAYER BUILDING BLOCKS

Practice reading these siddur words.
How many can you read correctly?
Practice reading them with a partner.
Put a check next to the words that you read correctly.

4 ___ וְשַׂמְּחֵנוּ	3 ___ שַׂבְּעֵנוּ	2 ___ קִדְּשָׁנוּ	1 ___ וְצִוָּנוּ
8 ___ וְהִגִּיעָנוּ	7 ___ וְקִיְּמָנוּ	6 ___ שֶׁהֶחֱיָנוּ	5 ___ עָלֵינוּ
12 ___ מַלְכֵּנוּ	11 ___ אָבִינוּ	10 ___ אֲבוֹתֵינוּ	9 ___ אֱלֹהֵינוּ
16 ___ עֵינֵינוּ	15 ___ יִשְׁעֵנוּ	14 ___ הָיִינוּ	13 ___ גוֹאֲלֵנוּ

CHALLENGE

Why do you think so many words in our prayers end with the suffix נוּ? _____

WRITING PRACTICE

Write the Words

Write the Hebrew word for *The Five Books of Moses.*

חֻמָשׁ

Write the Hebrew word for *Jews.*

יְהוּדִים

Write the Hebrew word for *Jerusalem.*

יְרוּשָׁלַיִם

Write the Hebrew word for *prayerbook.*

סִדוּר

Write the Hebrew word for *Kiddush.*

קִדוּשׁ

Write the Hebrew words for *Elijah the prophet.*

אֵלִיָּהוּ הַנָּבִיא

130

USING THE PHOTOGRAPH

What things in the photograph show that this is a holy occasion? [*ḥallot*, kiddush cups, *siddur*, *kippot*, everyone is dressed nicely, etc.]

THE LIVING TRADITION

At what other times do we recite Kiddush, besides Friday night? [**lunch on Shabbat; dinner and lunch on Rosh Hashanah, Sukkot, Simḥat Torah, *Pesaḥ*, and Shavuot**]

THE LIVING TRADITION קִדּוּשׁ

On Friday evening, after we light שַׁבָּת candles, we sing the קִדּוּשׁ over wine. The word קִדּוּשׁ means "making holy." When we sing the קִדּוּשׁ we thank God for making שַׁבָּת a holy day.

HOLIDAY BUILDING BLOCKS

Read the name of each holiday.

יוֹם כִּפּוּר	פּוּרִים	סֻכּוֹת
שָׁבוּעוֹת	חֲנֻכָּה	

HOLIDAY QUIZ

Write the Hebrew name of the holiday to answer the question: What holiday am I?

1 We read the מְגִלָּה. What holiday am I? **פּוּרִים**

2 We shake the lulav and eat in a small booth. What holiday am I? **סֻכּוֹת**

3 We celebrate the Giving of the Torah. What holiday am I? **שָׁבוּעוֹת**

4 We light the *hanukkiah*. What holiday am I? **חֲנֻכָּה**

5 We do not eat all day. What holiday am I? **יוֹם כִּפּוּר**

131

LESSON 23

Pages: 132–137
Key Word: מְזוּזָה
New Letter: ז
Alef-Bet Flashcard: 44
Word Cards: 73, 74, 75

REVIEW EXERCISE

Basketball

Drill the students on *alef-bet* flashcards 1–43 using a basketball theme. Divide the class into two teams. Each correct answer is worth two points. An incorrect answer moves the turn to the other team.

KEY WORD (מְזוּזָה)

If the doorpost to your classroom has a *mezuzah*, ask a student to point it out.

- What is inside a *mezuzah*? **[piece of parchment with the Shema written on it]**
- Why do we hang a *mezuzah*? **[The Shema tells us to love God, to keep God's commandments, and to put God's words on our doorposts.]**
- What do many Jews do when entering a room with a *mezuzah*? **[kiss the *mezuzah*]**

INTRODUCE THE NEW LETTER – ז

Print the following letters on the chalkboard and review them:

ו ז ו ו

Print a *zayin* on the chalkboard and introduce this new letter. How does the *zayin* differ in appearance from the other letters on the chalkboard. Display word card #73 and have a student point out the two *zayins* and then read the word.

READING PRACTICE

Return to the "basketball theme," calling on individuals to read each of the three lines and then having their teammates repeat in unison.

NOW READ & READ AGAIN

Call out a specific word, such as "line 3, fourth word" and have a student read that word. Have the student call out the next one, or continue to call them out yourself.

HERITAGE WORDS

On what occasions might it be appropriate to wish someone מַזָּל טוֹב?

What is a מַחֲזוֹר and on what holidays do we use a it? **[prayerbook used on Rosh Hashanah and Yom Kippur]**

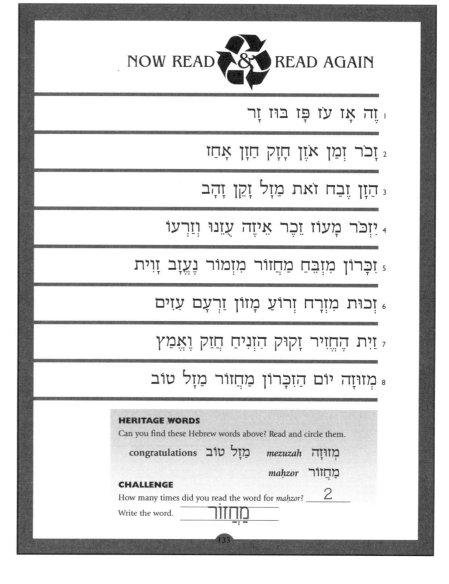

SEARCH AND CIRCLE

Have the students complete this exercise independently. Call on students at random to read each line aloud and to identify the Hebrew letter that should be circled.

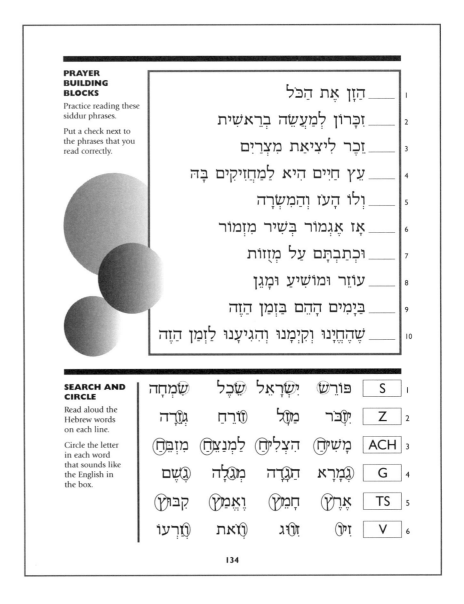

PRAYER BUILDING BLOCKS

Practice reading these siddur phrases.

Put a check next to the phrases that you read correctly.

_____ הַזָּן אֶת הַכֹּל 1

_____ זִכָּרוֹן לְמַעֲשֵׂה בְרֵאשִׁית 2

_____ זֵכֶר לִיצִיאַת מִצְרָיִם 3

_____ עֵץ חַיִּים הִיא לַמַּחֲזִיקִים בָּהּ 4

_____ וְלוֹ הָעֹז וְהַמִּשְׂרָה 5

_____ אָז אָגְמוֹר בְּשִׁיר מִזְמוֹר 6

_____ וּכְתַבְתָּם עַל מְזֻזוֹת 7

_____ עוֹזֵר וּמוֹשִׁיעַ וּמָגֵן 8

_____ בַּיָּמִים הָהֵם בַּזְּמַן הַזֶּה 9

_____ שֶׁהֶחֱיָנוּ וְקִיְּמָנוּ וְהִגִּיעָנוּ לַזְּמַן הַזֶּה 10

SEARCH AND CIRCLE

Read aloud the Hebrew words on each line.

Circle the letter in each word that sounds like the English in the box.

שִׂמְחָה	שֵׂכֶל	יִשְׂרָאֵל	פּוֹרֵשׂ	**S**	1
גְּזֵרָה	מַזָּל	זוֹרֵחַ	יִזְבֹּר	**Z**	2
מִזְבֵּחַ	לַמְנַצֵּחַ	הַצְלִיחַ	מָשִׁיחַ	**ACH**	3
גֶּשֶׁם	מְגִלָּה	הַגָּדָה	גְּמָרָא	**G**	4
קִבּוּץ	וְאֶמֶץ	חָמֵץ	אֶרֶץ	**TS**	5
זַרְעוֹ	זֹאת	זוּג	זִיו	**V**	6

134

NAME TAG

Read aloud the name of the Hebrew letter in each box and have your students circle the matching Hebrew letter on that line and then write the letter in the space provided.

WRITE THE LETTER

Have the students complete the writing practice exercises as in previous lessons. In print writing, ensure that the students are making the *zayin* correctly and are not writing it too similarly to a *vav*. In script writing, ensure that the students are not confusing the *gimmel* and *zayin*.

NAME TAG

Read aloud the name of the Hebrew letter in each box.

Circle the Hebrew letter named in the box. What sound does the letter make?

Write the letters you circled.

פ	ב	ס	פ	ת	כ	PAY	1
ע	שׂ	צ	שׁ	ל	SIN	2
ן	ד	נ	ו	ג	GIMMEL	3
פ	ב	ת	כ	פ	FAY	4
ק	שׁ	ס	צ	ם	SAMECH	5
ט	ע	ת	ד	מ	TET	6
נ	ו	ח	י	ר	YUD	7
כ	ח	ג	ת	ה	CHET	8
נ	ו	ד	י	ג	NUN	9
ס	שׁ	ג	ז	צ	ZAYIN	10

WRITING PRACTICE

Write the Letter

ז ז ז ז

Write the Words

Write the Hebrew word for *mezuzah*.

מְזוּזָה

Write the Hebrew words for *congratulations*.

מַזָל טוֹב

Write the Hebrew word for *maḥzor*.

מַחֲזוֹר

135

USING THE PHOTOGRAPH

- What is the girl doing in this photograph? [**putting up a *mezuzah***]
- How high is she hanging the *mezuzah*? [**top third of the right-hand doorpost, slanting toward the room one is about to enter**]
- How is she hanging the *mezuzah*? [**hammer and nails**]

THE LIVING TRADITION

Open up a *mezuzah* and show the parchment to the students. Point to the text of the Shema and Ve'ahavta. Explain that each *mezuzah* parchment is handwritten by a scribe, the same person who would write a Torah.

While the inside of all *mezuzot* are the same, making the outside cases has become a great art form. Have the students describe different *mezuzot* they have in their house or that they have seen. You may want to bring in a variety of *mezuzah* cases to display.

THINK ABOUT IT

The Torah teaches us to place the words of the Shema on the doorposts of our home to remind us that there is only one God and to show that the home is a place in which God is always present.

If your students know the tune for the paragraph after the Shema – *Ve'ahavta et...* – sing it with the students and then point out that the last sentence is the commandment about *mezuzah*. [**uchtavtam al mezuzot beitecha uvish'arecha – "and you shall inscribe them upon the doorposts of your homes and upon your gates."**]

THE LIVING TRADITION מְזוּזָה

The Hebrew word for "doorpost" is מְזוּזָה. The תּוֹרָה teaches that the שְׁמַע and the וְאָהַבְתָּ prayers should be placed "on the doorposts of your house and on your gates." These words are written on a piece of parchment which is placed inside a מְזוּזָה. We attach this מְזוּזָה to the doorposts of our homes.

THINK ABOUT IT

Why does the תּוֹרָה teach us to place the words of the שְׁמַע on the doorposts of our homes?

BE AN ARTIST

Draw a picture to illustrate each Hebrew word or phrase below.

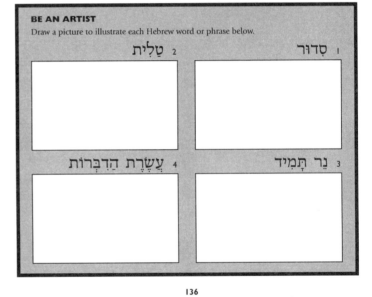

2 טַלִּית	1 סִדּוּר
4 עֲשֶׂרֶת הַדִּבְּרוֹת	3 נֵר תָּמִיד

136

CHECKPOINT

Choose from the following techniques:

1. Call on students to read the word in each box and provide the meaning if it has been learned.

2. Call out a box number at random and have a student read the word in that box.

3. Call out a Hebrew letter that has been learned and have students read all the words in the grid which contain that letter.

4. Call on students to read all words that conclude with a vowel. [2, 6, 7, 10, 13, 18, 22, 25]

FYI

Basic Checkpoint Technique

Use the Checkpoint to assess each student's progress. Listen to students read individually. Circle errors lightly in pencil in their textbooks. Reteach problem letters and retest students, erasing the pencil marks when they read the word correctly.

CHECKPOINT
Read the Hebrew word in each box.

סְגֻלָּה 4	שָׁבוּעַ 3	יִרְבּוּ 2	גְּאוּלָה 1
מְזוּזָה 8	צַוּ 7	אֵלִיָּהוּ 6	קָדוֹשׁ 5
כֻּלָּם 12	סִיּוּם 11	טוּבוֹ 10	חָמֵשׁ 9
חֲנֻכָּה 16	תַּלְמוּד 15	הַלְלוּיָהּ 14	בָּרְכוּ 13
רְפוּאָה 20	פּוּרִים 19	עֵצוּ 18	סֻכּוֹת 17
שׁוּבָה 24	יְרוּשָׁלַיִם 23	קוּמוּ 22	צוּר 21
		מְתֻקָּן 26	שִׁישׂוּ 25

137

LESSON 24

Pages: 138–142
Key Word: בָּרוּךְ
New Letter: ךְ
Alef-Bet Flashcard: 45
Word Cards: 76, 77

KEY WORD (בָּרוּךְ)

Hold up word card #6 (בְּרָכָה). Have a volunteer read and define it. Ask what word begins most *brachot*. [בָּרוּךְ] Display word card #76.

Have students name *brachot* that begin with the word *baruch*.

INTRODUCE THE NEW LETTER – ךְ

Have the students look at the *alef-bet* chart and identify all the letters they have learned that have a "partner" or family letter that is a final letter. [מ צ נ] Point to the *final chaf* and introduce it. As with the *chaf* and *het*, you may have to emphasize the "ch" sound.

How does the final *chaf* differ in appearance from the *dalet* and *final nun*?

READING PRACTICE

Have the students look at the key word in the textbook and ask a volunteer to read and define it.

Read line 1 in unison and then call on students individually to read the line. Have one student read line 2 and then have the entire class repeat the line in unison.

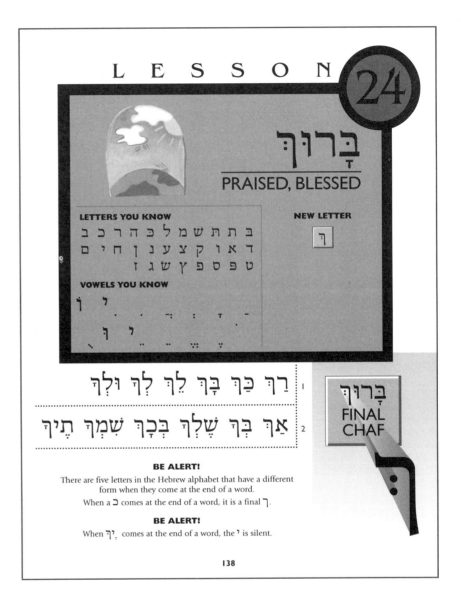

NOW READ & READ AGAIN

Draw a tic-tac-toe grid on the chalkboard. Divide the class into two teams. To place an X or an O on the board, the students must correctly read a line in the book.

HERITAGE WORDS

Name one of the kings of Israel. [e.g., **Saul, David, Solomon**]

Sing the song *David Melech Yisrael.*

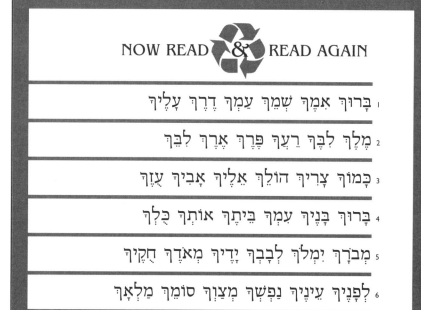

NOW READ & READ AGAIN

1 בָּרוּךְ אָמֵךְ שְׁמֵךְ עַמְּךְ דֶּרֶךְ עָלֶיךְ

2 מֶלֶךְ לִבֵּךְ רֵעֵךְ פֶּרֶךְ אֶרֶךְ לִבֵּךְ

3 כָּמוֹךְ צָרִיךְ הוֹלֵךְ אֵלֶיךְ אָבִיךְ עֻזֵּךְ

4 בָּרוּךְ בָּנֶיךְ עִמְּךְ בֵּיתֶךְ אוֹתְךְ כֻּלְּךְ

5 מְבֹרָךְ יִמְלֹךְ לִבְבְךְ יָדֶיךְ מְאֹדֶךְ חֻקֶּיךְ

6 לְפָנֶיךְ עֵינֶיךְ נַפְשְׁךְ מִצּוֹךְ סוֹמֵךְ מַלְאָךְ

7 מִצְווֹתֶיךְ קְדֻשָּׁתְךְ בִּשְׁלוֹמֶךְ אֱלֹהֶיךְ וַיְבָרֶךְ

8 תַּנָּךְ בָּרוּךְ וּבְלֶכְתְּךְ וּבְקוּמֶךְ וּבִשְׁעָרֶיךְ

HERITAGE WORDS

Can you find these Hebrew words above? Read and circle them.

praised, blessed   בָּרוּךְ

king, ruler   מֶלֶךְ

CHALLENGE

How many times did you read the word for *praised, blessed?* __3__

139

CLIMB THE LADDER

One option is to pair a stronger and weaker reader. After the two students practice reading the words to each other, have one student climb up the ladder and the other climb down. Record the amount of time it takes for each team to read correctly all the words and climb up and down.

BE ALERT!

Final ךּ is the only final letter that has a vowel.

Final ך is written ךָ or ךְ.

Read these words.

הַמְבָרֵךְ   בֵּיתֶךָ

CLIMB THE LADDER

Read each list of words.

Practice reading the words with a partner.

ך ךָ		כ כּ		כּ	
מֶלֶךְ	21	עַכְשָׁו	11	כַּלָּה	1
בָּרוּךְ	22	סֻכּוֹת	12	כּוֹס	2
לָךְ	23	בְּרָכוֹת	13	כָּל	3
עַמְּךָ	24	יִזְכֹּר	14	כָּשֵׁר	4
דֶּרֶךְ	25	יָכוֹל	15	כָּבוֹד	5
לְבָבְךָ	26	בֵּית-כְּנֶסֶת	16	כְּפוֹר	6
מִצְוֹךְ	27	לִכְבוֹד	17	כֹּהֵן	7
נַפְשְׁךָ	28	יְכַלּוּ	18	כֶּתֶר	8
מְאֹדֶךָ	29	חֲנֻכָּה	19	כָּלָם	9
אֱלֹהֶיךָ	30	שֵׂכֶל	20	כַּוָּנָה	10

140

WRITING PRACTICE

This is your final reminder that *Shalom Uvrachah* [the student's edition] is available in two versions—one for teaching print writing and one for teaching script. This universal Teacher's Edition can be used with either version. You can see samples of every letter in print format on page xiv.

WRITE THE LETTER

On the chalkboard, demonstrate the technique for writing the *final chaf*. Ensure that the students realize that the formation of the *final chaf* concludes <u>below</u> the ruled line. Also, if teaching print writing, check to ensure that the students are not making the *final chaf* too similarly to a *final nun* or *dalet*.

RHYME TIME

Have the students complete this exercise independently. Call on a student to read aloud each of the rhyming words on each line. Call on another student to read the word that does not rhyme.

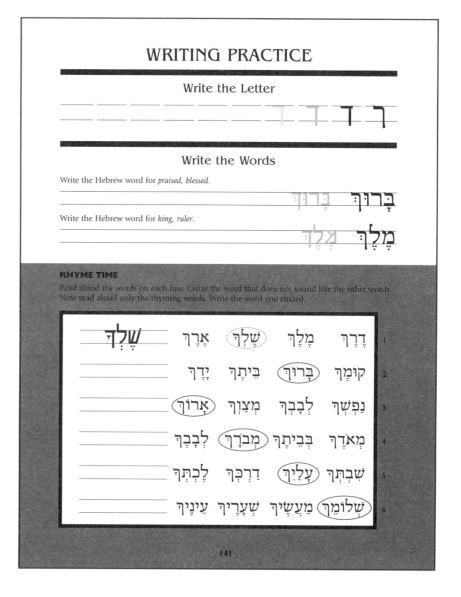

USING THE PHOTOGRAPH

- What holiday are the children celebrating? **[Rosh Hashanah]**
- How do you know? **[apple and honey, round ḥallah]**

THE LIVING TRADITION

Why do we say blessings over various things? **[to thank God for them; to stop and appreciate what we are about to bless]**

You have almost finished learning the entire *alef-bet*. Write a blessing thanking God for being able to reach that achievement.

THE LIVING TRADITION בָּרוּךְ

We have a special way of saying "thank you" to God for God's gifts to us. We say a בְּרָכָה—words of praise and thanksgiving to God. The word בָּרוּךְ, which means "blessed" or "praised," is the first word of many blessings. Below are the six words that begin some of the blessings we recite. Read these words, and then read the concluding phrases that follow.

בָּרוּךְ אַתָּה, יְיָ אֱלֹהֵינוּ, מֶלֶךְ הָעוֹלָם...

Praised are You, Adonai our God, Ruler of the world...

Put a check next to the בְּרָכוֹת that you read correctly.

Which בְּרָכוֹת do you know?

who brings forth bread from the earth.	١ ___ הַמּוֹצִיא לֶחֶם מִן הָאָרֶץ.
who creates the fruit of the vine.	٢ ___ בּוֹרֵא פְּרִי הַגָּפֶן.
who creates the fruit of the earth.	٣ ___ בּוֹרֵא פְּרִי הָאֲדָמָה.
who creates the fruit of the tree.	٤ ___ בּוֹרֵא פְּרִי הָעֵץ.
who creates many kinds of food.	٥ ___ בּוֹרֵא מִינֵי מְזוֹנוֹת.
by whose word all things come into being.	٦ ___ שֶׁהַכֹּל נִהְיֶה בִּדְבָרוֹ.
for keeping us in life, for sustaining us, and for helping us to reach this day.	٧ ___ שֶׁהֶחֱיָנוּ וְקִיְּמָנוּ וְהִגִּיעָנוּ לַזְּמַן הַזֶּה.

142

LESSON 25

Pages: 143–147
Key Word: אָלֶף
New Letter: ף
Alef-Bet Flashcard: 46
Word Cards: 78, 79

KEY WORD (אָלֶף)

Point to the *alef* on the *alef-bet* chart and have the students identify it.

Explain that *alef* is the first letter of the Hebrew alphabet. Teach the *alef-bet* song to the students and begin to teach the correct order of the letters.

REVIEW EXERCISE

Play the "Grandmother's Suitcase" game as described in #6 on page viii. Use flashcards #1–45. If you are not teaching the names of the vowels, have the students say the vowel sounds.

INTRODUCE THE NEW LETTER – ף

At the conclusion of the grandmother's suitcase game you should announce, "I packed my grandmother's suitcase and in it I put a *final fay*." Point out the final *fay* on the *alef-bet* chart and show its location on word card #78. Make sure the students can differentiate between it and the *final chaf*. Ask a volunteer to read the key word from the word card or in the textbook.

READING PRACTICE

Have students work in pairs reading each of the lines to each other. Listen as they practice, and correct any errors that you hear.

NOW READ & READ AGAIN

Have one student read aloud all the Hebrew words on a line, omitting one. Another student reads the Hebrew word that was skipped. This method encourages all the students to pay attention to their classmates reading.

NOW READ & READ AGAIN

1. נוֹף הַדַף חַף עָיֵף סַף חוֹף

2. חֹרֶף תֵּיכֶף עֹרֶף עָנָף כֶּסֶף שָׂרַף

3. שֶׁטֶף יוֹסֵף אָלֶף חָלַף כָּתֵף כָּפַף

4. מוּסָף צָפוּף קֶלַח זוֹקֵף קוֹטֵף לָעוּף

5. אָסַף נִשְׂרַף שָׁטוּף רָצוּף כָּנָף יָחֵף

6. עַפְעַף מְרַחֵף רוֹדֵף שָׁלוֹם זוֹקֵף כְּפוּפִים

7. מְצַפְצֵף לְהִתְאַסֵף לֶאֱסֹף הֶחֱלִיף לְשַׁפְשֵׁף

8. אָלֶף בֵּית וְצִוָּנוּ לְהִתְעַטֵף בַּצִיצִית

HERITAGE WORDS

Can you find these Hebrew words above? Read and circle them.

alef bet אָלֶף בֵּית   *alef* אָלֶף

CHALLENGE

Can you find the Hebrew name for *Joseph* in the lines above?

Write the line number. _____3_____

Do you know the story of Joseph, the son of יַעֲקֹב and רָחֵל?

Can you find the Hebrew word for *peace*? Write it here. שָׁלוֹם

READING RELAY

Another variation of this game would be to turn it into a writing relay. Have students come to the board with their book and write the words instead of reading them. Be aware that this could be time consuming.

READING RELAY

In column **א** Player 1 reads word 1. Player 2 reads words 1 and 2. Player 3 reads words 1 and 2 and 3. Continue the relay until Player 10 reads all ten words. Then play Reading Relay with the words in columns **ב** and **ג**.

ג		ב		א	
ף		פפ		פ	
כָּנָף	21	אֲפִיקוֹמָן	11	פָּסוּק	1
אֶלֶף	22	שׁוֹפָר	12	פּוֹקֵחַ	2
קֶלֶף	23	גֶּפֶן	13	פִּרְקָן	3
יוֹסֵף	24	סֵפֶר	14	פְּעָמִים	4
רוֹדֵף	25	תְּפִלָּה	15	פָּרְשָׁה	5
מְרַחֵף	26	מַפְטִיר	16	פּוּרִים	6
מוּסָף	27	תְּפִילִין	17	פֶּסַח	7
זוֹקֵף	28	לְפָנֵי	18	פְּרִי	8
תֵּיכֶף	29	מִשְׁפָּחָה	19	פֶּרֶךְ	9
אֹסֵף	30	תַּפּוּחַ	20	פָּנִים	10

CHALLENGE

Can you find the Hebrew word for *prayer*?

Which line is it on? ___15___ Write the word here. ___תְּפִלָּה___

WRITE THE LETTER

On the chalkboard, demonstrate the technique for writing the *final fay*. Ensure that the students realize that part of the letter is formed <u>outside</u> the ruled lines.

WRITING PRACTICE

Write the Letter

ף ף ף ף

Write the Words

Write the Hebrew word for *alef*.

אָלֶף אָלֶף

Write the Hebrew word for *alef bet*.

אָלֶף בֵּית אָלֶף בֵּית

SEARCH AND CIRCLE

Read aloud the Hebrew words on each line.

Three words on each line have letters that make the same sound as the English in the box. Circle the letters. Write the letters you circled.

CH	סוֹמֵךְ	לְפָנֶיךָ	תְּפִילִין	מַלְכוּתְךָ	1
CH	כָּבוֹד	בְּתוֹכֵנוּ	כְּמוֹכָה	זוֹכֵר	2
F	מַפְטִיר	תְּפִלָּה	פָּנִים	אֲפִיקוֹמָן	3
F	רוֹדֵף	בָּרוּךְ	מוֹסִף	זוֹקֵף	4
M	נוֹפְלִים	כְּפוּפִים	מְפַרְנֵס	הִתְפַּלֵל	5
M	מִצְוֹת	מִשְׁפָּטִים	שֵׁם	טוֹבוֹ	6
N	רָצוֹן	אֶרֶץ	הַזָּן	מָזוֹן	7
N	נֶאֱמָן	נַפְשְׁךָ	מִנְיָן	אָבִי	8
TS	חָמֵץ	אָמֵן	יַחַץ	עֵצָה	9
TS	יִצְחָק	צִיּוֹן	עֶלְיוֹן	צְבָאָם	10

BE ALERT!

Five letters have final forms.

Can you write the final form of each Hebrew letter?

נ ___ מ ___ צ ___ כ ___ פ ___

146

USING THE PHOTOGRAPH

What clues are there that the girl is standing in a religious school classroom? [*alef-bet* **chart, Hebrew writing on chalkboard, map of Israel, etc.**]

THE LIVING TRADITION/SIYUM HASEFER

Refer to page xix of this Teacher's Edition for some additional ideas to celebrate the conclusion of the students learning all the letters of the *alef-bet*. The *Siyum Hasefer* can also be delayed until the entire textbook has been concluded.

ALEF-BET CHART

After the students color in the five new letters on page 160, randomly say the names of Hebrew letters and ask the students to point to them on their charts. For variety, have the students take turns calling out the letter names.

THE LIVING TRADITION אָלֶף

אָלֶף is the name of the first letter in the Hebrew alphabet. The second letter in the Hebrew alphabet is בֵּית. That is why the name of the Hebrew alphabet is אָלֶף בֵּית. The English word *alphabet* comes from this Hebrew word. When we know the letters of the אָלֶף בֵּית, we can read Hebrew words, we can study the Torah, and we can pray from a סִדוּר.

> Think how many Hebrew words you already know!

LETTER NAMES

The names of the first ten letters of the Hebrew אָלֶף בֵּית are in the correct order. The letters are in random order. Write the correct letter above its name.

ג ח ה י ו ד ט ב ז

ה	ד	ג	ב	א
הֵא	דָלֶת	גִימֶל	בֵּית	אָלֶף

י	ט	ח	ז	ו
יוֹד	טֵית	חֵית	זַיִן	וָו

THE אָלֶף בֵּית CHART

You have learned five new letters in Lessons 20-25:

שׁ ג ז ך ף.

Turn to the אָלֶף בֵּית Chart on page 160.
Color in the new letters. You have learned every letter in the אָלֶף בֵּית.
Recite the complete אָלֶף בֵּית!

147

SPECIAL RULES

The following pages contain unusual reading rules and exceptions to standard pronounciation. These rules are like keys. They will help students unlock the door to accurate and fluent reading. Make sure the students understand each rule before proceeding to the next one.

After completing this section, the students will be able to read the prayer passages at the end of the Primer with speed and ease.

SPECIAL RULES

Rule #1
 אִי יְ יִ

When ְ , ִ , and אָ are followed by the letter י at the end of a word, say "EYE" as in "SHY" (שַׁי).

1 חַי אֲזַי שַׁי דַי סִינַי אוּלַי

2 אֵלַי מָתַי שְׂפָתַי שַׁדַי הֲלֹוַאי בְּוַדַאי

3 אֲדֹנָי אֱלֹהָי בְּחַיַּי מִצְוֹתַי חֻקוֹתַי רַבּוֹתַי

HERITAGE WORD

Can you find this Hebrew word above? Read and circle it.

live חַי

BE ALERT!

When וֹ comes after a letter that already has a vowel, it is pronounced וו.

מִצְוֹת = מִצְווֹת

מִצְוֹתַי = מִצְווֹתַי

148

Rule #2

וֹי וִֹי

When the vowel וֹ is followed by the letter י at the end of a word, say "OY" as in "boy." When the vowel וִ is followed by the letter י at the end of a word, say "OOEY" as in "gooey."

1 אוֹי גוֹי נוֹי הוֹי אֲבוֹי כוֹי

2 צִווּי קָנוּי עָשׂוּי רָצוּי גָּלוּי וִדוּי

3 פָּנוּי וַאֲבוֹי עֲלוּי בָּנוּי רָאוּי שָׁבוּי

Rule #3

יו יךָ

When יו or יךָ come at the end of word, the letter י is silent.

1 דְּבָרָיו אֵלָיו לְפָנָיו נִסֶּיךָ עֵינֶיךָ חֲסָדֶיךָ

2 עֲבָדֶיךָ מַעֲשֶׂיךָ אֱלֹהֶיךָ לְבָנֶיךָ וּבִשְׁעָרֶיךָ

3 מִצְוֹתָיו רַחֲמָיו אֱלֹהָיו בִּמְרוֹמָיו בְּמִצְוֹתָיו

Can you find these Hebrew words above? Read and circle them.

with God's commandments   בְּמִצְוֹתָיו

Your kindnesses   חֲסָדֶיךָ

149

Rule #4

יְיָ יְהֹוָה

In the prayerbook and in the Torah, God's name is written יְהֹוָה, יְיָ, or אֲדֹנָי.

We pronounce God's name "Adonai" (אֲדֹנָי).

Read the following סִדוּר phrases. Underline God's name each time you read it.

1. ____ אֲדֹנָי שְׂפָתַי תִּפְתָּח וּפִי יַגִּיד תְּהִלָּתֶךָ

2. ____ בָּרוּךְ אַתָּה יְיָ נוֹתֵן הַתּוֹרָה

3. ____ שְׁמַע יִשְׂרָאֵל יְהֹוָה אֱלֹהֵינוּ יְהֹוָה אֶחָד

4. ____ אַתָּה גִבּוֹר לְעוֹלָם אֲדֹנָי

5. ____ אַשְׁרֵי הָעָם שֶׁיְיָ אֱלֹהָיו

In the סִדוּר we find additional names for God.

Read the following סִדוּר phrases. The names for God are underlined.

God	1. ____ אֵל אָדוֹן עַל כָּל הַמַּעֲשִׂים
God	2. ____ וַיְבָרֶךְ אֱלֹהִים אֶת יוֹם הַשְּׁבִיעִי
my God	3. ____ אֲרוֹמִמְךָ אֱלֹהַי הַמֶּלֶךְ
our God	4. ____ בָּרוּךְ אַתָּה יְיָ אֱלֹהֵינוּ מֶלֶךְ הָעוֹלָם
God of	5. ____ אֱלֹהֵי אַבְרָהָם, אֱלֹהֵי יִצְחָק, וֵאלֹהֵי יַעֲקֹב

How well did you read?
Put a check next to the phrases that you can read correctly.

150

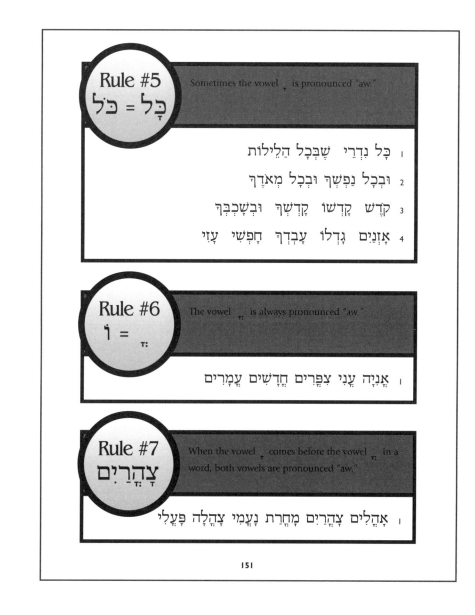

Rule #5

כָּל = כֹּל

Sometimes the vowel ָ is pronounced "aw."

1. כָּל נִדְרֵי   שֶׁבְּכָל הַלֵּילוֹת

2. וּבְכָל נַפְשְׁךָ וּבְכָל מְאֹדֶךָ

3. קֹדֶשׁ קָדְשׁוֹ קָדְשְׁךָ וּבְשָׁכְבְּךָ

4. אָזְנַיִם גָּדְלוּ עָבְדְּךָ חָפְשִׁי עָזִּי

Rule #6

וְ = ָ

The vowel ָ is always pronounced "aw."

1. אֳנִיָּה עֳנִי צִפֳּרִים חֳדָשִׁים עֳמָרִים

Rule #7

צָהֳרַיִם

When the vowel ָ comes before the vowel ֳ in a word, both vowels are pronounced "aw."

1. אָהֳלִים צָהֳרַיִם מָחֳרַת נָעֳמִי צָהֳלָה פָּעֳלִי

151

SHEMA (LINE 1)

In ancient days, people believed in many different gods – e.g., a rain god, a sun god, a god of thunder, etc. Our ancestors were different because they believed that One God creates and rules everything and everyone. The Shema is our central prayer that states our belief in one unique God.

Key and Heritage Words

shema

Yisrael

BARUCH SHEM... (LINE 2)

This line, recited quietly, states our belief that *Adonai* is the only true and eternal Ruler of the people Israel.

Key and Heritage Words

baruch

VE'AHAVTA... (LINES 3–12)

In this paragraph we are told to love God with all our being. We show our love for God by following God's laws and commandments and by teaching them to our children.

Key and Heritage Words

ve'ahavta – line 3

mezuzot (plural of *mezuzah*) – line 12

SELECTED READINGS

שְׁמַע / וְאָהַבְתָּ

1 שְׁמַע יִשְׂרָאֵל, יְיָ אֱלֹהֵינוּ, יְיָ אֶחָד.

2 בָּרוּךְ שֵׁם כְּבוֹד מַלְכוּתוֹ לְעוֹלָם וָעֶד.

3 וְאָהַבְתָּ אֵת יְיָ אֱלֹהֶיךָ

4 בְּכָל לְבָבְךָ וּבְכָל נַפְשְׁךָ וּבְכָל מְאֹדֶךָ.

5 וְהָיוּ הַדְּבָרִים הָאֵלֶּה

6 אֲשֶׁר אָנֹכִי מְצַוְּךָ הַיּוֹם עַל לְבָבֶךָ.

7 וְשִׁנַּנְתָּם לְבָנֶיךָ וְדִבַּרְתָּ בָּם

8 בְּשִׁבְתְּךָ בְּבֵיתֶךָ וּבְלֶכְתְּךָ בַדֶּרֶךְ

9 וּבְשָׁכְבְּךָ וּבְקוּמֶךָ.

10 וּקְשַׁרְתָּם לְאוֹת עַל יָדֶךָ

11 וְהָיוּ לְטֹטָפֹת בֵּין עֵינֶיךָ.

12 וּכְתַבְתָּם עַל מְזֻזוֹת בֵּיתֶךָ וּבִשְׁעָרֶיךָ.

152

BRACHAH BEFORE TORAH READING (LINES 1–6)

This blessing gives thanks to God for the privilege of being part of the people of Torah.

Key and Heritage Words

baruch – lines 2, 3, and 6
melech – line 3
torato (His Torah) – line 5
hatorah (the Torah) – line 6

BRACHAH AFTER TORAH READING (LINES 1–4)

This blessing praises God for the Torah's gift of true life to all who make it their own.

Key and Heritage Words

baruch – lines 1 and 4
melech – line 1
torat (Torah of…) – line 2
emet – line 2
hatorah (the Torah) – line 4

בִּרְכוֹת הַתּוֹרָה

1 בָּרְכוּ אֶת יְיָ הַמְבֹרָךְ.

2 בָּרוּךְ יְיָ הַמְבֹרָךְ לְעוֹלָם וָעֶד.

3 בָּרוּךְ אַתָּה יְיָ אֱלֹהֵינוּ מֶלֶךְ הָעוֹלָם,

4 אֲשֶׁר בָּחַר בָּנוּ מִכָּל הָעַמִּים

5 וְנָתַן לָנוּ אֶת תּוֹרָתוֹ.

6 בָּרוּךְ אַתָּה יְיָ נוֹתֵן הַתּוֹרָה.

1 בָּרוּךְ אַתָּה יְיָ אֱלֹהֵינוּ מֶלֶךְ הָעוֹלָם,

2 אֲשֶׁר נָתַן לָנוּ תּוֹרַת אֱמֶת

3 וְחַיֵּי עוֹלָם נָטַע בְּתוֹכֵנוּ.

4 בָּרוּךְ אַתָּה יְיָ נוֹתֵן הַתּוֹרָה.

153

V'ZOT HATORAH...

This prayer is recited as the Torah is lifted and dressed, at the conclusion of the Torah reading. It means, "And this is the Torah that Moses placed before the people of Israel to fulfill the word of God through Moses."

Key and Heritage Words

hatorah (the Torah) – line 1
Yisrael – line 3

ETZ ḤAYYIM HEE...

This prayer, taken from the Book of Proverbs, praises the Torah as our tree of life. It is recited as the Torah is returned to the ark.

Key and Heritage Words

etz ḥayyim – line 1
shalom – line 4

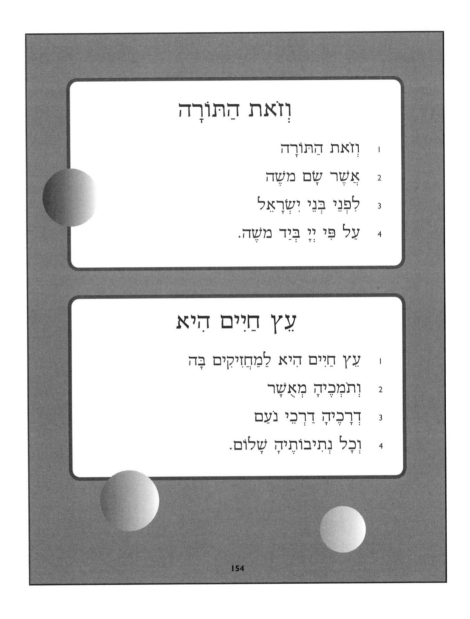

וְזֹאת הַתּוֹרָה

1 וְזֹאת הַתּוֹרָה

2 אֲשֶׁר שָׂם מֹשֶׁה

3 לִפְנֵי בְּנֵי יִשְׂרָאֵל

4 עַל פִּי יְיָ בְּיַד מֹשֶׁה.

עֵץ חַיִּים הִיא

1 עֵץ חַיִּים הִיא לַמַּחֲזִיקִים בָּהּ

2 וְתֹמְכֶיהָ מְאֻשָּׁר

3 דְּרָכֶיהָ דַרְכֵי נֹעַם

4 וְכָל נְתִיבוֹתֶיהָ שָׁלוֹם.

154

ALEINU

This prayer is part of the concluding section of every service. We are called to praise the God of all creation and to unite in harmony in our recognition of God.

Key and Heritage Words

melech – line 5

malchei ham'lachim (King of Kings) – line 5

hakadosh (the Holy One) – line 6

baruch – line 6

עָלֵינוּ

1 עָלֵינוּ לְשַׁבֵּחַ לַאֲדוֹן הַכֹּל

2 לָתֵת גְּדֻלָּה לְיוֹצֵר בְּרֵאשִׁית.

3 שֶׁלֹא עָשָׂנוּ כְּגוֹיֵי הָאֲרָצוֹת

4 וְלֹא שָׂמָנוּ כְּמִשְׁפְּחוֹת הָאֲדָמָה...

5 וַאֲנַחְנוּ כּוֹרְעִים וּמִשְׁתַּחֲוִים וּמוֹדִים
לִפְנֵי מֶלֶךְ מַלְכֵי הַמְּלָכִים,

6 הַקָּדוֹשׁ בָּרוּךְ הוּא...

7 וְנֶאֱמַר: וְהָיָה יְיָ לְמֶלֶךְ עַל־כָּל־הָאָרֶץ

8 בַּיּוֹם הַהוּא יִהְיֶה יְיָ אֶחָד וּשְׁמוֹ אֶחָד.

155

EIN KELOHEINU

Jews have been singing this praise of God for more than a thousand years. Although the words of this prayer are simple, they make an important statement about our belief in God: *ein keloheinu* – "There is none like our God."

Key and Heritage Words

baruch – lines 7 and 8
ke'malkeinu, che'malkeinu (like our King) – lines 2 and 4
le'malkeinu (to our King) – line 6
malkeinu (our King) – lines 8 and 10

MAH NISHTANAH

The Four Questions are important because by asking about the different parts of the seder, we are really asking about the reason for the entire *Pesaḥ* holiday. These questions force us to think about our people's Exodus from Egypt, as well as to examine areas in our own lives today where we may be enslaved.

Key and Heritage Words

ḥametz – line 1

umatzah (and matzah) – line 1

matzah – line 1

מַה נִשְׁתַּנָה

מַה נִּשְׁתַּנָה הַלַּיְלָה הַזֶּה מִכָּל הַלֵּילוֹת?

1 שֶׁבְּכָל הַלֵּילוֹת אָנוּ אוֹכְלִין
חָמֵץ וּמַצָּה. הַלַּיְלָה הַזֶּה כֻּלּוֹ מַצָּה.

2 שֶׁבְּכָל הַלֵּילוֹת אָנוּ אוֹכְלִין
שְׁאָר יְרָקוֹת. הַלַּיְלָה הַזֶּה מָרוֹר.

3 שֶׁבְּכָל הַלֵּילוֹת אֵין אָנוּ
מַטְבִּילִין אֲפִילוּ פַּעַם אֶחָת. הַלַּיְלָה
הַזֶּה שְׁתֵּי פְעָמִים.

4 שֶׁבְּכָל הַלֵּילוֹת אָנוּ אוֹכְלִין
בֵּין יוֹשְׁבִין וּבֵין מְסֻבִּין.
הַלַּיְלָה הַזֶּה כֻּלָּנוּ מְסֻבִּין.

157

HATIKVAH

Hatikvah was written at the end of the nineteenth century by the poet Naphtali Imber. It became the hymn of the Zionist movement in 1898 and the official national anthem of Israel upon the establishment of the State. The words to *Hatikvah* express the Jewish people's love for Israel and our longstanding dream to again have a Jewish homeland.

Key and Heritage Words

hatikvah – title and line 6
nefesh – line 2
Yehudi (Jewish) – line 2
tikvateinu (our hope) – line 5
virushalayim (and Jerusalem) – line 8

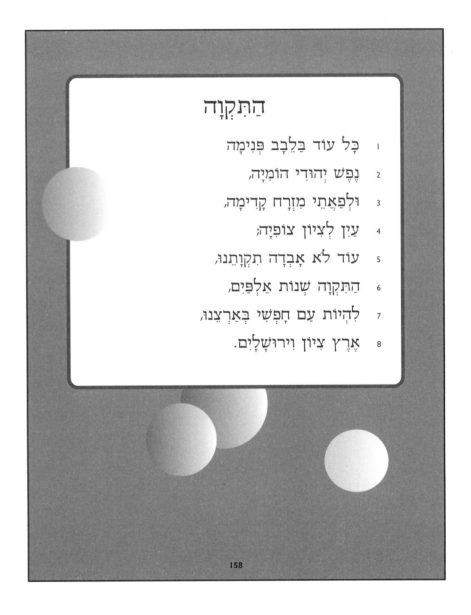

הַתִּקְוָה

1   כָּל עוֹד בַּלֵּבָב פְּנִימָה

2   נֶפֶשׁ יְהוּדִי הוֹמִיָּה,

3   וּלְפַאֲתֵי מִזְרָח קָדִימָה,

4   עַיִן לְצִיּוֹן צוֹפִיָּה;

5   עוֹד לֹא אָבְדָה תִקְוָתֵנוּ,

6   הַתִּקְוָה שְׁנוֹת אַלְפַּיִם,

7   לִהְיוֹת עַם חָפְשִׁי בְּאַרְצֵנוּ,

8   אֶרֶץ צִיּוֹן וִירוּשָׁלָיִם.

158

HERITAGE WORD LIST - מִלּוֹן

א
אָדָם	the first human, man
אַהֲבָה	love
אֱלֹהִים	God
אֵלִיָּהוּ הַנָּבִיא	Elijah the prophet
אָלֶף	alef
אָלֶף בֵּית	alef bet
אָמֵן	Amen
אֱמֶת	truth
אֲפִיקוֹמָן	afikoman
אֲרוֹן הַקֹּדֶשׁ	the Holy Ark

ב
בַּר מִצְוָה	bar mitzvah
בָּרוּךְ	praised, blessed
בְּרָכָה	blessing
בַּת	daughter
בַּת מִצְוָה	bat mitzvah

ה
הַבְדָּלָה	havdalah, separation
הַגָּדָה	haggadah
הַמּוֹצִיא	blessing over bread
הַמּוֹצִיא לֶחֶם	Who brings forth bread
הַפְטָרָה	haftarah
הָרַחֲמָן	the Merciful One (God)
הַתִּקְוָה	the Hope, national anthem of Israel

ו
וְאָהַבְתָּ	and you shall love

ח
חַג שָׂמֵחַ	happy holiday
חַי	live
חַלָּה	hallah, braided bread
חָמֵץ	leavened food
חֻמָּשׁ	Five Books of Moses
חֶסֶד	kindness

ט
טַלִּית	tallit, prayer shawl

י
יְהוּדִים	Jews
יוֹם טוֹב	holiday, festival
יְצִיאַת מִצְרַיִם	Exodus from Egypt
יְרוּשָׁלַיִם	Jerusalem
יִשְׂרָאֵל	Israel

כ
כַּלָּה	bride
כִּפָּה	kippah, skullcap

ל
לְחַיִּים	to life

מ
מְגִלָּה	scroll
מָגֵן דָּוִד	Shield of David, Jewish Star
מְזוּזָה	mezuzah
מַזָּל טוֹב	congratulations
מַחֲזוֹר	mahzor
מֶלֶךְ	king, ruler
מַלְכָּה	queen
מִנְיָן	minyan, ten Jewish adults
מַצָּה	matzah
מִצְוָה	commandment
מָשִׁיחַ	Messiah
מִשְׁפָּחָה	family

נ
נָבִיא	prophet
נֶפֶשׁ	soul
נֵר תָּמִיד	eternal light

ס
סִדּוּר	prayerbook
סֵדֶר	seder
סֵפֶר תּוֹרָה	Torah scroll, Five Books of Moses

ע
עִבְרִית	Hebrew
עֲלִיָּה	aliyah, going up
עֵץ חַיִּים	tree of life
עֲשֶׂרֶת הַדִּבְּרוֹת	Ten Commandments

פ
פֶּסַח	Passover

צ
צְדָקָה	justice
צִיצִית	fringes on tallit

ק
קַבָּלַת שַׁבָּת	Welcoming Shabbat
קִדּוּשׁ	Kiddush
קָדוֹשׁ	holy
קַדִּישׁ	Kaddish

ר
רֹאשׁ הַשָּׁנָה	Jewish New Year

ש
שַׁבָּת	Shabbat
שַׁבָּת הַכַּלָּה	the Sabbath Bride
שַׁבָּת הַמַּלְכָּה	the Sabbath Queen
שַׁבָּת שָׁלוֹם	a peaceful Shabbat
שׁוֹפָר	shofar
שָׁלוֹם	hello, good-bye, peace
שִׂמְחַת תּוֹרָה	Rejoicing of the Torah
שְׁמַע	hear
שֶׁמֶשׁ	helper
שָׁנָה טוֹבָה	Happy New Year

ת
תּוֹרָה	Torah, teaching
תְּפִלָּה	prayer